The experts loved it!
Read what they said about *Please Make Me Cry:*

"Simply a great book . . . a tremendous love story . . . every reader of this book will be moved to tears and laughter."
　　　　—FROM THE
　　　　　FOREWORD BY DAVID WILKERSON

"I believe in miracles and the pages that follow tell about one."
　　　　—FROM THE
　　　　　FOREWORD BY KATHRYN KUHLMAN

PLEASE, MAKE ME CRY!

COOKIE RODRIGUEZ

with

BETTY SCHONAUER

Whitaker House

PLEASE MAKE ME CRY

Cookie Rodriguez
Cookie Rodriguez Street Church Academy
P.O. Box 17266
Dallas, TX 75217

ISBN: 0-88368-042-4
Printed in the United States of America
Copyright © 1974 by Whitaker House

Whitaker House
580 Pittsburgh Street
Springdale, PA 15144

11 12 13 14 15 16 17 18 19 / 06 05 04 03 02 01 00 99 98 97 96

To the women in my life:
  My grandmother, Nina
  Ruth Cowgill
  Sharon Webb
  Dagmar Oldfield
  Pauline Bernstein
  My mother
  And all who have come to New Life For Girls.

"But a woman that feareth the Lord, she shall be praised."   —Proverbs 31:30b

And to:
  My husband, Demi
  My oldest son, Dondi
  And all those whom the Lord has used to help us.

CONTENTS

FOREWORD

by David Wilkerson

Please Make Me Cry is simply a great book! Cookie's story is told with warmth, humility, and tremendous spiritual insight. Her ministry and life include a bit of Kathryn Kuhlman's charisma, some of Nicky Cruz's forcefulness, and a whole lot of Jesus.

This is a tremendous love story, and Cookie's husband, Demi, is a gracious man of God. Without a doubt, every reader of this book will be moved to tears and laughter and—more important—will be drawn closer to Christ.

I do hope this book enjoys a very wide circulation. It is worthy of a place on the best seller list. This is one true story you cannot put down until you have read it all at one sitting. I heartily recommend it as one of the best I have seen involving a life story and a conversion.

FOREWORD

by Kathryn Kuhlman

Please Make Me Cry is a true story which is quite likely to make you cry. Whether you are a parent or teen-ager this book will open your heart and mind to one of the great social evils threatening to undermine the very fabric of America.

Here is a book that does far more than pose a problem, for it shows clearly the answer. This is not the trite material of a cheap novel but rather it speaks eloquently with the anguish of thousands of young people caught in a sordid life they unsuspectingly wandered into. If you are one who may be called to help them find a way out, here's a book with that clear ring of truth coming through on every page. It puts you into their shoes. It will reach into your heart to help you love and care for even the most miserable. I believe in miracles and the pages that follow tell about one.

PREFACE

This is really the story of *two* women. They share the same name, but beyond that resemblance ceases. The first of these women is a total stranger to me—I never met her. The second has become truly my sister.

The story of the first woman *has* to be told. It is painful, ugly, and at times shocking; but it reveals the real truth about the degradation of society's toughest, most "incurable" problem—the female drug addict—in a way that mere statistics never can.

The story of the second woman should be shouted from the housetops! It contains the joy, the love, the hope that are available even to the outcast.

In truth, this is also the story of a Third Party Who fills these lives with His presence. The hand of God has clearly been upon these women from the beginning. To Cookie Rivera—gang member, pothead, drug addict, prostitute—He didn't exist. To Cookie Rivera Rodriguez—wife, mother, and ministering angel to scores of drug-addicted young women—He is *all*, the very source of her life.

I want to introduce you to Cookie as she *was* and as she *is*—and to the God Who continues to create in her, and in others like her, new life, new hope, and an endless supply of love.

Betty Schonauer

PART ONE

Chapter 1

NOT EVEN DEATH

"Who's doing all that screaming?"

"Oh, that's Mrs. Rosario, Dr. Chang. She's the grandmother of that Puerto Rican girl they brought in DOA* an hour ago. We can't convince her that her granddaughter is actually dead, and she won't sign the papers to have the body taken to the morgue. The girl was only twenty-two."

"*That* little bag of bones? She looked twice that age!"

"Yeah—well, I guess she had it pretty rough—"

"Would it help if I talked to the grandmother?"

"Well, you can try, but Dr. Weinstein couldn't get through to her. She doesn't speak English. Carmen, our aide, can interpret for you. She's trying to talk to her now. They're in room 2—first door on the right."

The scene in the treatment room was as chaotic as it sounded. On the table, partially hidden by a sheet, a puny body lay ominously still. Another tiny form hovered by the table with bony fingers clutching at that lifeless figure. Despite the efforts of the uniformed aide who was attempting to soothe the woman, her wailing and shouting persisted as Dr. Chang stepped into the room.

"There now, Mrs. Rosario, that's not doing any good. Screaming won't help your granddaughter."

* Dead on arrival.

"*¡Ayudela, doctor! ¡No deje que mi Irmita muera! ¡Ella es buena! ¡Tiene que ayudarla! ¡Por favor!*"

"She says, 'Help her, doctor! Don't let my little Irma die! She's a good girl. You've got to help her! Please!' "

"I'm afraid it's too late for that. You can see that she isn't breathing or—

"Wait a minute! Her feet are still warm! Dead junkies don't have warm feet! Nurse! Sam! Give me a hand here, will you?

"Stand back, Mrs. Rosario! We're going to try to give your Irmita back to you."

By the time this decision was made to fight for my life, at least eight hours had passed—eight hours since I had taken the fix that had proven to be a near-fatal overdose. You couldn't blame Manuel for leaving me in that condemned building where we'd gone to take our fix. He had done the best he could for me. You could usually count on a fellow junkie to try all the tricks to revive you if you took an overdose—salt-water injections, then milk, for instance. If nothing works, you can't expect a guy to hang around. No one wants to be found with a junkie's corpse.

Three days after my admission to the hospital, I awoke in a confusion of sounds, sights, and sensations. Many voices could be heard in the distance, along with other unfamiliar, muffled sounds that gave me no clue to my whereabouts. I was lying on my back—somewhere. I opened my eyes and saw a ceiling that was too white for a tenement, but cracked and peeling in a comforting, familiar way. The glare from the lights that dotted the ceiling made my eyes smart, and I turned my head to avoid them.

"Now what is that?" I asked myself. On a silver pole beside my bed hung a large bottle containing a clear liquid which flowed downward through a piece of transparent tubing connected to the bottle. Then I became aware of the coolness in my immobilized right arm.

"What is this nonsense?" I recognized the familiar feeling of a needle in my vein, but I missed the warmth that should have accompanied it. "An IV bottle!* I'm in the hospital! Oh, man! Now how did I get here?"

As my mind struggled to recapture some memory of prior events, I became aware of a giant-sized headache and an extreme feeling of nausea. A sudden cramping in my middle made me instantly aware that, whatever else had happened, I had not had a fix in some time.

"Must have ODed† again. That's getting to be a habit these days. This one must have been a doozie. Why couldn't it have finished me off?' It would have made things easier all the way 'round." But I had *not* died. I was very much alive, and a live junkie sooner or later zeros in on only one idea.

"I need a fix! Got to get out of here!"

My condition at that point was officially listed as "serious," and those IV fluids were really life-supportive. But they weren't feeding my system the food it craved. With my left hand, I fumbled with the wads of tape until I finally got to the needle. It was the right instrument, all right, but its clean sterility did not make up for its grave inadequacies. I pulled it out of my vein, sending a slow stream of droplets onto the gray floor.

On unsteady legs, I groped my way to the steel closet by the door and yanked it open. Familiar dungarees and a faded shirt hung limply inside, and a jacket grey with dirt fell at my feet. By then I felt re-

* Bottle used for intravenous feeding.
† Short for "overdosed."

ally dizzy and very weak. I had to lean against the cool metal of the locker as I pulled my clothes on. Driven by the strongest motivation I knew, I steadied myself to stroll casually out of the room to the nearest exit sign. In a few minutes I was out in the street, surrounded by the anonymity of New York City at night.

The invisible radar that guides a junkie to his fix was already at work. "Feet, just get me to Fox Street. Ah, there's the bar! Someone ought to be there by now. Gonna be OK in just a minute!"

Once inside I spotted the man I wanted to see. "Hey, Joe! What d'ya say, man? Got some for me?"

"Oh, man! It can't be *you!* You're supposed to be dead! Cookie? Is it really *you?*"

So they'd all gotten word that I'd finally done myself in. Guess everyone was feeling pretty bad about it too.

"I'm *fine!* Really! I just need a fix is all. What d'ya got?"

Later, as I was coming down from that high, I began to notice that the stares I was getting weren't all friendly. In fact, no one seemed terribly glad to see that I was still alive. What was wrong?

"Not even death wants you, Cookie!" was what they said.

I hadn't really thought about it like that. "Hey, that's right! I've been turned down by death itself. What's *wrong* with a person who can't even die?"

There had been many times before when I thought I'd hit rock bottom and there was no farther to fall. But I was always wrong! There seemed to be no end to the downward trip I'd begun. And this was the worst by far. Rejected by death, I was now shunned by the other junkies, my "friends." These junkies were the closest thing to a family I had now, and this incident seemed to have cut me off even from them. No avenue of help remained open. I'd tried everything. "God! Why can't I *die?*"

I had not meant to call on God. It had been a curse, not a prayer. Nevertheless, within a few short months He began to answer this question by showing me why I was to live.

Chapter 2

FROM THE START

I was born Irma Marina Rivera thirty-two years ago in Caguas, Puerto Rico. Caguas was a typical Puerto Rican town with low-lying stone buildings and an imposing Catholic church in the center of the town plaza. This central plaza was clean and orderly. As a child I thought it beautiful.

My family, however, lived in the poorer section of town, the *barrio*—my country's equivalent of a ghetto. It was not beautiful. In fact its ugliness is still painful to recall. Home for me was an unpainted wooden shack without electricity or running water, crowded among many others like it. The interior of the house was one large, dingy room with no partitions for privacy. Only one family in our barrio had an electric refrigerator; we didn't even have an icebox. Our cooking was done on a kerosene stove. The street outside our house was unpaved, and the windows lacked glass or screens. In dry weather, clouds of dust settled on the furniture, dishes, and cooking utensils. In wet weather, enormous mosquitoes zeroed in on us like squads of miniature dive bombers, whether we happened to be indoors or out. All the children of the barrio played barefooted in the streets, and all had bellies swollen by hookworm infestation.

At the time of my birth, my mother was a child herself—just thirteen years old. My father, an older man of seventeen, had chosen to escape life and fatherhood a few months before my birth by drinking a bottle of Lysol.

So I was really raised by my grandmother. I called her *Abuelita,* "little grandmother." She was very thin, and her skin was swarthier than mine. Her dark, kinky hair was always drawn tightly into a bun—a hair style which served to accentuate her dominant feature, the piercing, deepset eyes that expressed her every feeling. She was very demanding, and her tongue was so sharp that she could carve me down to nothing in a matter of seconds. As the head of our household she commanded respect from all the family: me, my mother, and my aunts and uncles who were her grown children. Widowed in her twenties, she had never remarried. With no man to make life any easier, she was used to shouldering responsibility and giving the orders. She supported me out of her meager earnings as a cook and cleaning lady; so I felt an obligation to obey her. While I was little, what Abuelita told me to do, I *did.*

I think I must have known she loved me, but we never spoke of love. All affection in my family was expressed by the physical touch—a gentle pat or a hearty hug. Abuelita did the best she could to nurture me, but she never managed to instill in me the assurance that I was acceptable to anyone outside my home. I never felt I belonged anywhere. With a mother who seemed more an adolescent problem child than a parent to me, and with no father figure at all, I felt set apart by my family structure long before I became aware of other shortcomings.

I also felt estranged from life by poverty. Poverty was always a significant part of my existence. Being born to poverty in Puerto Rico brought with it the feeling that life offered no alternative. Those born in poverty would die in poverty.

I was more sensitive to this poverty than the other children of the barrio. I was the only one in my neighborhood who had the privilege of attending the private Catholic school in the center of town. All my classmates there were children of the wealthy families in town. Early in life, I was able to observe the subtle differences in the treatment accorded the child of a wealthy banker and that meted out to the grandchild of a woman who cooked and cleaned for the priests. Because my grandmother was employed by the school, she paid no tuition for me; the money that came from the other children's families kept the school running. By the time I was in the second grade I had come to expect a snub from the other children before it came; and to defend myself, I was growing a tough exterior.

I began to hate the children in that school. I hated anyone who could be considered "better" than I was merely because she was born into a family with more money. I even hated the nuns for their slights, real and imagined. Even though I did well in my studies I was never singled out for special favors. A mistake by another child never seemed to be noticed as much as the mistakes I made. If any effort was made to teach the Christian principle of turning the other cheek, I didn't get the message. My habit of striking back at the world with anger and hatred had its roots deep in my childhood experiences.

Unconsciously, I began to accept society's evaluation of me as valid. I would have denied it vigorously, but deep within I was beginning to think of myself as inferior. I expected very little from myself and almost nothing from life. Only two dreams struggled to exist in the poor soil of my early years.

They were the only goals I can remember having as I grew up.

The first of these goals might have been shared by ninety-nine percent of all Puerto Rican girls in the fifties. I wanted to wear white on my wedding day. Wearing a white wedding dress was, to my contemporaries and me, the visible evidence of purity and self-respect.

"They'll *all* know that I'm really a nice girl then. Everyone will have to admit that I'm as good a person as anyone." I entertained such thoughts frequently, dreaming of the new respect that society would give me. A kid from the barrio was just as nice as anyone else. I'd show them myself.

The other goal grew out of my success as a student. I wanted to be a teacher when I grew up. I suppose this was just a continuation of my quest for acceptance and respectability. Teachers were admired and respected. You *were* someone if you were a teacher. The lack of money for advanced education would have to be overcome. I was going to be a teacher.

Meanwhile Abuelita was making her own plans. Like many other poor people in Puerto Rico, my grandmother looked to New York City as a place of great opportunity. For as long as I could remember, Abuelita had talked of putting aside enough money to get to New York, where life was easier. America was the land of opportunity. A person might have a sense of hopeless poverty in Puerto Rico; but in New York City one could work one's way up, right to the top.

An uncle and his family, as well as other more distant relatives, had already emigrated when I realized how serious Abuelita was about our moving to New York. The glowing reports she received from these family members increased her determination. By the time I was 12½ she had managed somehow to save our plane fares from her small earnings. Almost before I knew it, we were seated in a Constellation headed north.

"Here we go, Irmita! We are going to take off!" My grandmother's excited chatter rose above the piercing noise of the engines as the plane shuddered and vibrated its way into the sky. "Aren't you excited? We are going to be there today. New York City! You'll see, it will be better there. More money! We might even get rich! And you'll get your education and be a teacher. You'll see, Irmita!"

I could not put my own feelings into words. Why *was* I reluctant to go? Didn't I *want* a new start? What had been so great about our miserable life in Caguas, anyway?

Perhaps I only was reacting to change the way *any* adolescent, particularly such an insecure one, might have reacted. Perhaps the dread I was feeling was just fear of the unknown. Or perhaps I had sensed already that this move was not going to be a step up in the world for me.

Chapter 3

NEW WORLD, NEW WAYS

Streets paved with gold and money growing on trees were what our family's enthusiastic reports had led us to expect of New York City. But those golden streets sure looked like black asphalt and gray cement to me! As for money trees—well, just plain *trees* were hard enough to find. Money was scarcer yet. I quickly decided that I hated New York.

Because we could speak no English when we first arrived, we were rather at a loss to find a place to live. Moving into a one-room furnished apartment with my uncle, two aunts, and four cousins was the easiest way to put a roof over our heads. In spite of the deplorable overcrowding in our apartment (one small cousin had to use a bureau drawer as a bed), our address was the Lower East Side of Manhattan—at that time a rather respectable neighborhood. Upper-middle-class families occupied lovely apartments in buildings nearby. To Abuelita it seemed a pretty good start.

She was quick to enroll me in a Catholic school near our apartment. She had brought me to America to get an education; so an education I was going to get.

At this first school I drew a certain amount of curious interest as the only Spanish-speaking child in the whole student body. That part of the city had very few Puerto Rican families, and none had enrolled a child in the Catholic school. So my inability to communicate in English fascinated my classmates and gave me a certain degree of status. A couple of children, a brother and sister, were very friendly and walked to and from school with me. We played games together as they invented ways of communicating with signs and gestures. I began to feel an acceptance and an acceptability I had not felt in the school in Caguas. I began to think, "perhaps this new country will be OK after all. Maybe here money and position are not so important."

Almost as quickly as I had dared to think such a thought I found history repeating itself. Coming to our apartment one day to invite me out to play, my friends discovered our deplorable, crowded condition. Horrified, they told everyone what they had seen, and immediately I was ostracized. To their eyes we lived like animals, and I was therefore viewed as somehow less than a person. I already knew how to retreat behind a wall of silence and hostility. The ways of this new world were not so different after all.

Meanwhile my scholastic endeavors were completely blocked by the language barrier. "The gibberish they speak here—no one can make any sense of it! How do they understand each other? I'll *never* learn this language!" Such were my thoughts during my first weeks at school. I had been frustrated to find myself demoted from the seventh to the sixth grade; but without language skills I could not even keep up with the studies on that level. This inability to achieve added fuel to the fires of frustration and anger burning within me.

Unexpected help finally came from a nun who knew a smattering of Spanish. She had actually visited my country at one time and had some appreciation of my frustration with the language barrier. When she offered to teach me English in after-school sessions, I quickly accepted. She had hopes that I would in turn help her improve her Spanish. I studied intensely with her for one hour a day after school. Within three months I had a beginning grasp of the language. I seriously doubt that Sister's Spanish had made similar gains.

Even such rudimentary English as I then possessed made me the family interpreter. We were emboldened to search out a new and larger apartment for the nine of us to share.

I'm sure we were cheated. My English was not up to bargaining with tenement landlords, and our fresh-from-Puerto Rico "banana look" was no help. Abuelita had to pay $300 to "buy" the place before we could occupy it for $100 a month rental. Rent did not include any utilities and was fairly high for the heart of East Harlem at that time.

Nevertheless the apartment seemed a palace to me! Five whole rooms! I could hardly believe I would be sharing my room with only one person—Abuelita. The "palace" lacked heat and, like all the drab and dreary tenements around it, was in a state of disrepair. But it sure beat living nine to a room!

The very best part of our new home, however, was the fact that it was located in Spanish Harlem—Little Puerto Rico, as it was called. We felt right at home. Everyone on the streets looked and talked just like us. Several of our neighbors, in fact, came from our town of Caguas back in Puerto Rico. We began to feel that we really belonged in this new place.

However, I was given no chance to enjoy this sense of homecoming. Abuelita was still thinking of my education as she picked out another Catholic school for me. I was back in the classroom once more.

This school, St. Cecilia's, gave me an education far broader than Abuelita had envisioned. She remembered the Catholic school in Puerto Rico, where the finer families had their children educated. Nothing could have prepared her, or me, for St. Cecilia's.

It looked exactly like the ugly old tenements around it: dismal, gray, and falling apart. The worn floors were warped and cracked, and poor lighting did nothing to disperse the burdensome gloom. I was shocked to see writing all over the walls. In Puerto Rico the walls of the school had been spotless. But at St. Cecilia's, four-letter words, hearts with names or initials, and slogans and jokes about the nuns filled the walls with their vulgarity. I was horrified!

Student behavior reflected the same crudeness. Girls smoked openly in the restrooms, boys and girls necked furtively in doorways, and filthy language could be heard constantly in the crowded corridors. I could hardly believe my eyes and ears my first day there!

"These can't be the 'nice' kids, can they? No decent girl would smoke in public!" Without thinking, I applied upper-class Puerto Rican standards, the ones that had been so unfairly applied to me earlier, to this new world with its entirely different ways. I soon found that young ladies whose dating was carefully chaperoned were not to be found in this country—at least not at St. Cecilia's.

It was while I was attending St. Cecilia's that I received my introduction to gangs. The gang members were nasty kids who made a conscious effort to look and act tough. They were easy to identify. They used the current slang expressions like, "Put it there, baby!" and, "Gimme five" almost as identification badges. Fights between members of rival gangs broke out frequently in the school or on the school grounds. I did everything I could to steer clear of them. Reasoning that if I didn't bother the gangs, they wouldn't bother me, I carefully avoided getting mixed up with gang members. I was afraid of that whole scene.

I had been at St. Cecilia's about a month when our family position altered drastically. Abuelita's bankroll, the money she had brought with her from Puerto Rico, had run out. The language gulf made it difficult for her to find work as a menial. My uncle had begun to drink heavily; and, family or not, we represented a drain on his resources. In this country it was he, not Abuelita, who was considered the head of the household. He threw us out.

We spent one night sleeping out-of-doors in the Bowery before one of the ghetto families took us into their home and introduced us to the wonderful world of welfare. Since we had no worldly possessions and no income, we certainly qualified for this kind of relief. Our names were added to the welfare rolls for the first time.

At that time welfare recipients were not permitted to work. If you took a job, no matter what the pay, welfare payments ceased. Since no one could actually exist on the meager welfare allowances, employment was necessary, but it had to be kept a secret. My grandmother took work wherever she could find it; but to the welfare investigators, our means of support were invisible. We had begun to recognize what was necessary to survive in the ghetto, where normal social structures had begun to crumble. There were a lot of tricks to be learned if we were going to make it here.

Perhaps it was her determination to survive, the glint of steel I detected in her, which led to my calling Abuelita by a different name. She no longer seemed like my *little* grandmother. Although still

29

small in stature, she was big in purpose. She intended to make it in this new world. The working of angles for survival had already begun. Her most frequent employment at this time was as a babysitter, and the children she kept called her *Nina*, the Spanish equivalent of "Nana." Abuelita became *Nina* to me too.

Chapter 4

THE LANGUAGE OF VIOLENCE

"Hey, Spick! Where'd *you* come from? You right off the boat?"

The language of our new neighborhood in West Harlem was not as familiar and friendly as that in the Puerto Rican section we had left. In this racially mixed neighborhood, blacks and Puerto Ricans lived in tense coexistence and mutual hatred. I had hated before: the children in school back in Caguas, the nuns I felt had slighted me, the "friends" who had dropped me so fast when they saw my home, my uncle when he threw us out. But now hate was given a color. It was black.

There was no logic to my people's feud with the blacks in the ghetto. Both peoples shared equally in the misery of slum living. Neither could be considered the "haves" or the "have nots." But extreme poverty breeds peculiar reasoning. Society at that time seemed to be telling the Puerto Rican immigrants that we were an inferior people, but we couldn't buy that indictment. We knew that many of our countrymen *were* rising above initial disadvantages of poverty to become educated, respected members of American society. I guess those of us who were not yet making it looked around for a reason for our failure, someone to blame. The blacks seemed hostile to our presence and they were easy to identify. As simply as that, the black people became my enemy.

Once we had settled in West Harlem, Nina's thoughts naturally turned once again to my schooling. I somehow managed to talk her into letting me transfer into a public school, where the English requirements were not as stringent as in St. Cecilia's. I was able to qualify for the seventh grade on the basis of my age and school performance in Caguas. It felt great to escape from St. Cecilia's. But Booker T. Washington Junior High School offered no improvement.

This school reflected and magnified all the racial tensions of the neighborhood. Hatred defined by race smoldered continually and often flamed over trivial incidents. There were gangs at this school too. But they were drawn along racial lines and seemed committed to all-out war with one another.

Because I was not a member of any gang, I was quite vulnerable to abuse and harassment. Black girls went out of their way to trip me in the halls or knock books out of my hands. Since I was a "Spick" without gang protection, I was fair game for anyone. I was always afraid, and my fear kept me from fighting back. Somehow I managed to put up with a lot of tormenting for a long time.

I did have a few friends among the other Puerto Rican girls who, like me, had no gang affiliation. We usually conversed with each other in Spanish, which the blacks could not understand. Our English was just as unintelligible to them as our Spanish; but our use of a language that plainly excluded them was a source of real annoyance.

It was the language gap that eventually precipitated the kind of confrontation I had tried to avoid. Among the many black girls in my class who took pleasure in taunting me was a particularly offensive one named Norma. Norma was a big girl—rather dull-witted, but loud and vulgar. My friends and I said she had a "bad mouth." I usually managed to ignore her comments to me. My fear at least was a sensible fear; Norma was almost twice my size.

But the day came when I could not resist a retort to one of her taunts. It was really a mild reply, but my heavy accent obscured the meaning. Norma thought she heard the word, "nigger," and that was a fighting word to her. Without warning she jumped me right in class and began to shove and punch me. For once, my instinct for self-defense conquered my fear, and I fought back without thinking. In the struggle I managed to knock her glasses off. When they fell to the floor I stepped on them, crushing them with my heel.

Although the teacher managed to break up the fight, Norma and I both knew the battle had not really ended. I had gained a personal enemy who was not likely to let the matter drop.

With the return to calm, my courage melted away at once and was replaced by the familiar knot of fear deep within. Norma had a gang to back her up, but I had no one to come to my defense. Why hadn't I just let her ugly remarks pass, as I usually did? Why hadn't I kept my own mouth shut?

My fears proved valid. At the close of school, I was met at the exit by Norma and a dozen other black girls, Norma's gang.

"Why did you do that to my 'sister'?"

"Hey, Spick, that ain't no way to treat my 'cousin'!"

Norma's gang had suddenly become close relatives who presented a solid wall before my path. There was no way to escape.

I felt the blood drain from my face and a cold

clamminess settle on my body. My stomach churned, and great iron bands seemed to immobilize my arms and legs. My entire body tensed in fear as the gang began to encircle me. Suddenly Norma reached out and pushed me. The other girls followed her lead, and the verbal taunts were replaced with a lot of shoving. Long-suppressed anger and hatred boiled up from within and melted the cold fear. I began to push back.

The beating they gave me probably did not take as long as it seemed, but they were thorough. I was bloodied from many cuts and swollen with bruises when I stumbled home to Nina that day.

I had seen no one during the fight except my assailants, and no one had tried to help me. But the battle had not gone unobserved. I had fought hard against terrible odds. The fury of my defense had surprised everyone, including me. My fears had found release as I discovered a new way to express myself—in violence. The word was out even before I had reached home: "That skinny Rivera girl is something else in a fight!" My days of running from the gangs had ended.

Chapter 5

THE DIAMONDS

The street had a language all its own.

"Hey, baby! Where's the action?"

"At Indio's."

"His old lady gonna be out all day?"

"Well—she ain't exactly been invited to the set, man!"

"What's the word? Thunderbird! What's the price? Thirty twice! Oh, man, are we ever gonna get *high* today!"

A knowledge of current street slang was essential for understanding other gang members. At that time, "action" usually meant either a "rumble" or a "set"—a fight or a party. Gang members often cut classes at school to have sets at each other's homes. They'd dance the "grind" to loud rock-and-roll music, do a little necking, and get high on cheap wine. And naturally, nobody planned to have a set when his "old lady"—his mother—was going to be around. When it was time for the parents to come home, they'd clean up the apartment and take off. We felt really cool about pulling off a party like that.

I was fourteen years old when I was accepted as a "deb," a member of the girls' branch of a gang. My gang, the Diamonds, was composed of Puerto Rican boys, ranging in age from twelve to eighteen. The Diamonds had about a hundred guys in the local membership and boasted additional turfs all over New York. They also had a reputation for toughness without mercy. Anybody who messed with a member of the Diamonds was going to get hurt.

Such was my fame after my fight with Norma and her gang that I had been accepted immediately into the Diamonds without the usual initiation. My ability to remain tough in a fight had already stood the test. Within a short time I was acknowledged as unofficial leader of the girls. I became gang-toughened and hardened almost overnight.

Since the primary function of the Diamonds, like that of every other gang, was to protect its members and its "turf," or territory, we were constantly in battle with some other gang over one petty dispute or another. In fact, if we weren't having a party, we were usually fighting. Gang life tended to operate almost exclusively in these two dimensions.

Often a fight was initiated by an incident at school, such as my altercation with Norma. The "offended" party would take his grievance to the gang's "war counselor," who determined whether this insult should be tolerated or avenged. Almost always the decision was made to fight for the honor of the gang. If another gang was involved, the war counselors of both gangs then got together to determine where the battle would take place and what weapons would be used. This sounds quite civilized and organized, but there was never real honor among the gangs. Frequently one gang would show up with zip guns as weapons when knives and chains had been chosen. The injuries inflicted in such battles were often serious and, all too frequently, fatal.

I was considered a good fighter. This did not stem from any great love of fighting on my part. Quite the contrary: I never lost my fear. Rather it was fear that

36

made me alert in a fight—fear of being cut in the face, fear of getting shot by the unpredictable bullets fired from a zip gun. Fear sharpened my wits. I fought aggressively to keep myself from being the one hurt. In an earlier day I had looked for and anticipated snubs and hurts from others. As a gang deb I looked for and anticipated injury before it came. Feelings had become action. Figuring that the "best defense is a good offense," I saved myself from serious injury many times by injuring first.

Meanwhile Nina and I were not seeing eye to eye on anything. She steadfastly refused to comprehend that her little Irma could be mixed up in the gangs. She was forever bugging me about my clothing or behavior: "Irmita, you wear a dress like a nice girl, not those dungarees. You want to look like one of those girls who runs with the gangs?" Or perhaps, "You're such a good girl, Irmita. You are going to *be* somebody some day. I am so proud of you!"

I could not stand her blind stupidity. What would it take to make her accept reality? I'd come home all busted up from a fight and she'd want to call the police to complain that "thugs were beating up Irmita." The *police* she wanted! *No one* in our neighborhood ever called the police, for *anything*.

I began to feel contempt for this grandmother of mine. Nina was living in a dream world, while I was growing tired of pretending to be something I wasn't. I gradually stopped asking permission to go out when the gang had "business" to attend to. I just stayed away from home more and more. The old habits of respect and obedience for my grandmother as head of my family were broken. The gang became my family.

Perhaps one reason Nina remained blind to what I had become was that I continued to do well scholastically. I managed to keep school and gang in separate

37

compartments of my mind. I might act tough at school or get into arguments, but still I could envision myself gaining real respect from the world as a teacher. Since I was able to achieve good grades with minimal effort, I remained in the first section of my class all through junior high.

One incident, however, should have alerted Nina to what was happening to me. I was in the eighth grade at the time. A school monitor, who happened to be a black, tried to keep me from entering the lunchroom by the wrong line. He was just doing his job, but I felt I had a reputation to live up to.

"What'd ya *mean* I can't come this way?" I asked. "Who says so? *You*, niggerboy?" I might have been content just to drop it there—but I was with Pedro, a member of the Diamonds. When it looked as though I would back down, Pedro pulled out a zip gun and waved it in the monitor's direction. "No, kid," he proclaimed, "if you want to go this way, you can *go* this way. Don't take no lip from no nigger!"

Intending only to frighten the boy, Pedro fired a bullet at the floor. But it richocheted off the polished surface and hit the monitor in the arm.

Even in our gang-torn school this was an extraordinary event, and an alarming one. Questioned first by school authorities and then by the police, I was eventually released. But Pedro, who had confessed to having brought and fired the gun, was booked and taken to jail.

I learned something then about gang loyalty. I was never given a chance to explain what had actually happened. Word got back to the president of the Diamonds that I had squealed on Pedro to save my own neck. Because this was the worst crime a gang member could commit against a fellow member, I knew the meaning of fear once again. This time what I

38

feared *most* was retaliation from my own gang members.

I confessed my fear to Nina and she agreed to move to a new neighborhood seven blocks away. Absurd as it may seem, this was as good as a move out of New York to those of us who never ventured outside our own turf. We stayed out of sight of the gang until Pedro got the word back that I had not been the cause of his arrest. Only then did I return to my gang. *My* gang, indeed! I had learned a valuable lesson about the permanence of gang ties. Although I stayed with the Diamonds, I could never seem to regain a really secure sense of belonging.

I also began to look at the deb scene from a different perspective. I had always been more of a loner than the other girls in the gang. I had excused myself from getting involved with any of the guys because I felt that, as one of the leaders, I needed their respect more than I needed their romantic interest. But I was beginning to recognize that this was just a cover for my feeling that any girl was dumb for getting involved with a guy and turning up pregnant at thirteen or fourteen. I would not have admitted then to continuing dreams of a white wedding dress, but my personal standards remained basically unchanged. I felt I was too smart to get messed up with any fellow.

Nevertheless, I continued to run with the gang for protection and for kicks. Playing hooky to go to the all-day movie theaters in Times Square or to a set in someone's home, talking tough in four-letter words at all times, and being increasingly evasive and abusive of Nina and others in authority were basic to my life style. I was a typical, street-hardened gang deb.

Even though the shooting incident had earned me a two-month suspension from school and was played up by the newspapers, Nina was still able to come to my defense. I was just at the wrong place at the wrong time. Who could blame me for *that?* In vain did the rest of my family try to convince Nina that I was no good. Nina was much too stubborn and loyal to Irmita. But I finally got into one scrape that really opened her eyes—one where there was no one else to blame.

All the teachers knew I was a gang member, but most hoped that eventually I would "find myself" and give up my wild ways. They recognized my native intelligence and were encouraged with my fairly good scholastic achievements. There was one teacher, however, who just could not tolerate gang members—especially girls. She taught social sciences. I used to tell myself she had to be a Communist, the way she picked on Puerto Ricans. She was forever putting me down in front of the entire class. One day she singled me out to be punished by standing in front of the room with my back to the class. I rebelled and refused to obey her.

"You won't defy me!" she shouted, pulling me by the arm.

She shouldn't have touched me. I had not let anyone push or shove me for almost two years, and tugging on my arm set off a chain reaction that could not be stopped. I pushed her back and kicked sharply at her legs with the metal taps on my shoes. Despite the fact that I had drawn blood with my kicking, she continued to pull on me, screaming all the while for help. I began cursing loudly. For a little old lady she did not give up easily.

I was taken to the office and the police were called in. They booked me for assaulting the teacher; but since I was only 14½ they did not quite know what to do with me. The court decided to send me to the psychiatric ward at Bellevue Hospital for evaluation. It was assumed that I was taking drugs. I was a known gang member and drugs were readily available to us on the streets. It was thought that drugs might be the cause of my violent behavior. The climate of my existence was one of deprivation, hatred, and rejection. With such a background, I couldn't believe they needed a "reason" for my violence.

The doctors were thorough in their examination of me, even down to the internal exam Nina had requested to see if I was still a virgin. To Nina, people were either all good or all bad. It had taken her a while to wake up to what I had become—but once her suspicions were awakened, she thought the worst of me. And how I hated her for that! Nothing she could have done would have aroused my resentment as questioning my virginity had done. When it came to reasons for personal pride, that was really all I had left. Nina was as surprised as the authorities to learn that I was still a virgin and showed no evidence whatever of drug usage. After another two-month suspension I was allowed to return to classes.

Meanwhile it seemed that the whole gang was literally going to pot! Whereas before we'd gotten high on Thunderbird wine and cheap whisky, now it was marijuana that turned us on. I became as big a pothead as anyone. When I was high on pot, I could discard my tough act and be as silly as the rest. It was such a relief to be able to laugh and act crazy that I soon found myself dependent on marijuana to get through a day.

But an even worse addiction was taking root in the gang. I first noticed it when some of the guys didn't want to fight. They seemed drowsy, half asleep all the time. Then I realized that they were "nodding," or high on heroin. It was the beginning of the end of the Diamonds.

I was very sure that I wanted no part of heroin. I didn't need to get messed up that way. I could still make something out of my life; I had a good head. Who needed a bad scene like heroin addiction? Certainly I didn't.

Chapter 6

DISAPPEARING DREAMS

I suppose curiosity is the reason most often given for trying heroin the first time. "I just wanted to see what it was like. I knew I wouldn't get hooked just trying it once." Very similar statements have been elicited from a lot of junkies over the years. It was this same curiosity that finally got me.

I had a friend, a boy I knew from my home town in Puerto Rico. In fact he got his nickname, *Caguita* ("Little Caguas") from the city of our birth. I considered Caguita almost one of my family, and Caguita was a junkie. I was with him one day when he needed a fix.

"Man, oh man! I gotta get somethin' soon, and I got nothin' left to trade. How 'bout lettin' me borrow your radio?"

That little portable radio was the nicest thing I owned. Even Caguita could not expect me to let him have that for *nothing*.

"Tell you what," I replied. "You take it, but you bring back some stuff for me. I want to try just a snort."

Within seconds of pushing the pungent powder into each nostril and sniffing, or "snorting," deeply, I was flying higher than I'd ever imagined possible. My skin began to itch all over and I started vomiting, but the reality of these circumstances escaped me. I felt

43

really free of all cares—totally detached. Despite the beauty of that detachment, I was sufficiently impressed with the power of that drug to be too scared to try snorting again for several months.

At this point two events combined to set my dreams of ultimate respectability completely at rest.

First I lost my dream of becoming a teacher. Despite my good overall grade average, which had kept me in the upper sections of the eighth and ninth grades, I was not permitted to go on to an academic high school where I could prepare for higher education. I had failed algebra, a subject I found impossible to grasp. My understanding of the English language still lacked appreciation of abstract symbols. It is possible that if I had shown any initiative or interest in getting help in this area, I would have received some tutoring. Perhaps I could then have passed the subject. But I was too proud. I was a respected and feared gang deb, with other kids looking up to me. I couldn't admit to needing the help of any square old algebra teacher. My desire to be a teacher, though still very much alive, had to be well hidden from the sarcasm and sneers of my gang.

So I totally missed the boat. Failure in this one subject was enough to shunt me off to Central Commercial High School, an all-girls vocational school. With the broken pieces of a lifetime ambition at my feet, I promptly lost *all* interest in my studies. I knew I had missed my chance to become a teacher, and I could think of no substitute goal.

"No sense pretending," I thought. "You blew it! You'll never get to college now. Might as well give up on this stinkin' school scene!"

My usual method of handling disappointment and hurt came to the fore. I became a real discipline problem in school—playing hooky more and more,

44

fighting other students when I was at school, and being foul-mouthed and abusive to the teachers. The hatred I was expressing to the world was really self-hatred. I was angry at *myself* for missing the opportunity. But no one around me got a glimpse of my disappointment. Instead they saw a fifteen-year-old gang girl wearing a chip on her shoulder and angry with the world at large.

The last dream to die was my white wedding dress. And it was destroyed in the most senseless way. I still thought of myself as too clever to get mixed up with a guy, so I continued to avoid any kind of close attachment to fellows in the gang. But I still was very much a part of the sets, the drinking, and the smoking of pot. This combination was eventually my undoing.

To my somewhat critical eye, Miguel was not even good-looking. He was too stocky for one thing, and he had a bad complexion. About all he had going for him was his age. He was twenty-four. An ex-soldier, he had the appeal of an older, more worldly-wise man. It was something of a feather in my cap that at fifteen I was able to interest a guy so much older.

We had been drinking wine, smoking pot, and necking. That was really dumb, making out with a guy who outweighed me by at least a hundred pounds, when both of us were high enough not to know the score. Before I could cool him off he had overpowered me. It was so stupid and so unnecessary.

So that eliminated my last bit of pride in myself. The white wedding dress had been just a symbol, but it had stood for my feeling that within me was a person of worth, someone respectable and honorable, that no one else knew about. When I lost touch with the symbols of that person, the teacher and the virgin, I lost the last of my illusions about the "real me"

45

emerging. That respectable part of me didn't exist after all.

"Who have you been kidding anyway?" I taunted myself. "Some big deal *you* are! Thinking you are so different from all the other dumb slobs around here, huh? Well, take a good look. You're no smarter than all the rest. And you're gonna end up like all the others!"

And I set out to prove that my self-evaluation was true. I drank excessively and came to school high on pot. I began dabbling with heroin on weekends, and soon had the inflamed and eroded nasal membranes of the habitual "snorter." If I ever looked at a nice girl with any envy, it depressed me so much that I'd require more booze and drugs to help me forget.

I had a bad habit of wanting to take company with me on my drug trips. When I made the mistake in school of turning some girls on to pot who were not really part of the gang and drug culture, it created waves of concern among the teachers. Again I found myself shunted from the school office to the police, and then back to Bellevue Psychiatric Ward.

What could they do with an incorrigible girl like me? In many ways I was far older than my fifteen years. I had grown crafty and tough from scores of gang fights. I had endured poverty all my life and had observed death at close range in street battles. I had accustomed myself to accepting relief from this life through alcohol and drugs. I was not yet a junkie, but it seemed clear that I was well on my way.

Eventually the psychiatrists, my probation officer, good old Nina, and an academy-award acting bit on my part saved me from incarceration in a reformatory. The psychiatrists felt that I was not really delinquent, just disturbed. With their help I could be salvaged. My probation officer concurred. Nina cried and carried on about how I was not really a bad girl, just unlucky. She still saw in me what I had decided could not exist. She insisted I could still "be somebody" if I was given a few breaks. My part was to dress myself as "Miss Average Teen-Ager" in skirt and bobby socks, and to force some convincing tears to flow as I faced the judge. He was sufficiently impressed with my act to rule out the reformatory. Instead I was sentenced to treatment at Rockland State Hospital for ninety days, followed by a period of probation.

I had missed prison by inches. I felt I was pretty lucky to have gotten off so easily.

Chapter 7

NO LESS A PRISON

Rockland continued to look like a good deal to me as the bus carrying me there passed through its iron gates. A cold wind whistled briskly outside, and droplets of rain were hitting the window; but the spacious, tree-covered grounds of the hospital seemed pleasant and peaceful to me. Only the clanking sound made by the gates as they were shut behind us gave any hint of what awaited me.

Escorted by attendants, I was transferred to a shuttle bus and driven past several dark brick buildings with iron bars guarding each window. Women ran to the enclosed porches calling obscenities to the attendants and, oblivious to the cold, lifted their dresses to attract attention. The peacefulness of the surroundings was broken by their shrill cries and hysterical shouting.

Peace returned when we entered the Female Admission Building. Efforts had been made to decorate the place tastefully, and the effect of the muted colors and soft lighting was a relaxing one. It was my last contact with civilized living for many months.

Uniformed women questioned me. I was brusquely passed from one impersonal cog in the administration machinery to another until, at last, I found myself in ward 21.

Ward 21 was dark and gloomy. It also stank! When

the door was unlocked to admit me, female attendants who were as large and husky as the average man took over. One of them took me to my room, a drab sliver of space just big enough for one narrow cot. The room contained no other furniture. A window too high to provide a view of the outside was protected by cold gray bars of steel. This room was to be my prison for the first week at the hospital. Ward 21 was the "violent ward," where those who had committed acts of violence, such as murder and torture, were sent. Until it was established just *how* violent a patient was, she was kept isolated from the rest of the ward population.

Another burly matron stepped inside the door and stripped me down to shivering flesh. The ugly, gray-green nightgown she gave me had to be worn against the skin with no underwear. The idea slowly dawned on me that Rockland was going to be no picnic.

"This can't be happening to me! I'm supposed to be here to get treated for emotional disturbance. This isn't any way to treat a kid like me! In ninety days I *will* be crazy!" Thoughts of this sort were racing through my mind. I discovered, however, that I had no choice whether to go or stay. Rockland was no less a prison for me than any reformatory might have been.

The days I spent locked in that room were long and lonely. I saw no one except the attendants who brought me meals or medication, and those anonymous eyes that occasionally observed me through the little peephole in the door. I had plenty of time to reflect on my life up to that point. I reviewed the lost dreams and the disappointment I'd been to Nina.

It was easy to see that I'd made a mess of things, but solutions were harder to come up with. Reasoning was made all the more difficult by the screams and weird grunts of the other patients that sifted through the walls. The fear that was within me at that time stemmed from real desperation. "Only ninety days of this," I tried to reassure myself. "If I can just stay out of trouble, I'll be OK. Thank goodness I'm not *really* crazy!"

But life inside an institution like Rockland was as difficult for an angry, hostile teen-ager as life on the outside had been. I soon realized that the old pattern of striking first to avoid possible hurt was only going to get me into deeper trouble.

Eventually I was considered "safe" enough to be allowed out with the other patients. A routine established itself. At eight in the morning they unlocked my door and I ate breakfast with the other patients in a large dining room. Then we were herded into the showers, where we were washed down by those mannish attendants. This remained a disgusting ordeal for me. For those who could not care for themselves a mass scrubbing was obviously necessary, but I could not understand why I was not permitted to wash myself. Following our shower we were locked in the "day room" until lunch. Afternoons were more of the same. Then, following dinner, we were locked up in our own rooms once again.

The sameness of this unvarying routine really got on my nerves. The other patients were usually repulsive to watch, with their weird ways and ridiculous mannerisms. The stench of human wastes filled the day room at all times, adding another assault on the senses. I hated the twisted beings I saw around me: that woman in her thin see-through nightgown with nothing underneath who was continually jumping up to recite poetry, and the fanatic with the Bible who preached endless sermons to no one in particular. I found it impossible at times to tolerate them. Whenever I slapped one of the other women in the face to shut her up, the attendants looked the other way. They were often as annoyed by a patient's behavior as I was, and relief from any source was welcomed.

It amazed me that eventually I made an adjustment of sorts to the routine. Perhaps it was the emergence of another gang structure that helped keep me sane. I discovered that other gang members were receiving the same sentence from the courts that I had. Incorrigibles from all over the city were being "rehabilitated" by admission to the state hospital. We identified one another quickly and soon resumed our old ways within the confines of the hospital walls. Gang warfare was naturally limited, but we could usually get a good fight going at mealtimes, the gang of one ward against the gang from another. Of course our behavior did not go unnoticed, and I was reported often to the conduct board. My ninety-day sentence was soon extended.

Another helpful diversion was furnished by visits to my psychiatrist, Dr. Philips. Fresh from residency and full of genuine concern for his patients, he seemed to me to be the most delightful human being who had ever taken an interest in me. My weekly visits to talk with him in his office became the high spots of my existence. He was so good-looking and so concerned about me. I did everything I could to be cooperative.

In fact, I was *too* cooperative. In order to keep him from being bored or discouraged with my case, I invented traumatizing events from my "past" and presented fresh data whenever his interest seemed to wane. My fantasies earned me the attention of two additional psychiatrists that Dr. Philips called in as consultants in my case. With all the conflicting stories I was feeding them, they found it difficult to come up with a definite diagnosis. But at least they all agreed that I did not belong on the violent ward.

My new ward, a nonviolent one, allowed me more freedom of movement. But it was no less boring and depressing. I continually begged Dr. Philips to prescribe some drugs to help make life bearable. He eventually tried both "uppers" and "downers" in his course of treatment. I used them both to get stoned whenever I could save up a big enough supply.

I also found other means of tolerating the intolerable. From one attendant I could coax an occasional glass of milk laced with Scotch. Then hard-core drug addicts who were admitted to kick the heroin habit became a possible source of a little heroin to snort. Many had an "old man"—a guy they lived with—who would keep a supply coming in as best he could through visiting privileges. For a little money, they'd cut me in. And finally I conned Nina into bringing me Cokes that were at least half whisky. She cooperated only because I told her I'd stay off drugs if she would just bring me a little pain-killer.

Life could have been almost bearable, if it had not been for my temper. Too long I had allowed it free rein. Now I could not keep from getting into fights. I was not even smart enough to stay at peace with the attendants.

One memorable night the evening attendant caught me out of bed after "lights out." Exasperated by my chronic breaking of rules, she needed little excuse to report my misdemeanors.

"Ah, there's our little Miss Smart Stuff. Big bad gang girl! Can't obey the rules, can't follow orders like everyone else. When are you gonna wise up, baby, and get it through your thick Puerto Rican skull that this isn't gang city in here? You're not the

52

one in charge here. *I'm* giving the orders now and you gotta *take* 'em!"

"Oh, go to hell, Lois!" I snapped back.

"That's right, sweetheart, get sassy! You just hate to put up with us, don't you? Well, let me tell you, you're gonna *have* to put up with us a long time the way you're heading! Don't think this will go unreported."

"Get out of here. I'm *going* to bed. You can beat it now. You don't have to stand around here flapping your jaws!" I was practically shouting. No one got away with talking that way to *me*.

"You bet you *are* gonna go to bed! But now you've got yourself one more black mark to keep you locked up!"

That *did* it! I was not at all happy with the repeated extensions of my ninety-day sentence and something inside me snapped under her taunting. Enraged, I wanted to strike out at her, but I knew that hitting an attendant was most unwise. So I hurled my clenched fist at the wall behind me. At least I *thought* it was the wall. I didn't even notice the sound of breaking glass, or the cut it made: the warmth of the blood coursing down my arm was my first clue that my fist had gone through the window beside my bed instead.

"Now you've *done* it, sister! That window will cost you!"

This final jab broke the last of my control. Screaming obscenities, I lunged toward her. I was stopped by another attendant, who took me to the infirmary to have my lacerated arm stitched; but the violence of my reaction was considered cause enough for an additional "therapeutic" measure—the cold pack.

Reserved for the most violent patients, the cold pack is designed to slow down body functions and reactions by cooling. Most truly agitated mental patients can be calmed by such a method. It only served to agitate me further.

Stripped naked and bound in wet sheets on a bed of ice with the winter wind blowing through the open window above me, I was sure I would go insane through this night-long ordeal. I heard myself calling for my mother, the mother I barely knew and had seldom seen. "Oh, man, I am really going crazy!" I told myself. "Maybe if I try talking out loud I can keep my mind straight. No—I'll try singing. How about 'Jingle Bells'? It sure is cold enough!"

Throughout the cold night I sang "Jingle Bells" and Christmas carols in English and Spanish and tried to imagine I was having a beautiful Christmas. I managed to survive the torture, but I was almost incoherent the next morning. When they took me out of the cold pack, I could hardly walk or talk. Immediately, they put me into a straitjacket. A whole day of having my arms bound tightly to my body completed the dehumanizing process the cold pack had begun.

Before that experience, I had been able to feel a little compassion or tenderness toward some of the patients. I had hated some, but others aroused my pity. I'd even felt something akin to friendship with some of them. After that day I was no longer capable of feeling anything but all-consuming hatred for everyone. I decided I'd never ask anything from anyone again. I would fight Rockland every inch of the way, all alone.

So it happened that my original ninety-day sentence turned into more than a year of agony before I was brought before the directing board again. Dr. Philips told them that he thought I was ready to make another try at living in society, and I assured the board that I would make it this time.

"Yes, sir, I've learned my lesson all right. No more

54

messing around for me! I'm going back to school and make something of myself." I was able to make such a statement sound very convincing. Actually I was only *half* acting for the benefit of the board. I really *would* have liked to get my life straightened out, only nothing had really changed. My past was still there, the future held no new promise. Now I carried the additional scars of the year's incarceration at Rockland. Where could I go from there? Rehabilitation had not touched me. I had not learned obedience and self-control at Rockland. Instead I'd become less cooperative and more independent than ever. No one seemed to know quite what to do with me.

Where could I go from there? Finding no alternative, I went back to the familiar streets of the ghetto, straight from the semi-violent ward at the state hospital.

Chapter 8

MAINLINING AND MOTHERHOOD

I found Nina full of plans when I returned home again. We would start over: we'd move to a new neighborhood—this time *really* far away, in the Bronx. She had already made all the arrangements, so I only had a couple of weeks to become reacquainted with the old turf before being whisked off to escape the "bad environment that had caused my problem," as my grandmother liked to think. Nina was still as bossy as ever and still quite sure she knew what Irmita needed.

I did make two significant discoveries in the brief time before we moved.

First of all, school was definitely *out* for me. As reluctant as my high school was to take me back, they had finally taken a chance and allowed my return to classes. At 16½ I felt foolish in the tenth grade again. All the crowd I had run with before had quit school when they hit sixteen, so I found none of my old companions. I tried playing the role of serious student, but it seemed pointlessly stupid. It was too much bother. I knew I'd never be a teacher. Further, I would be nineteen years old before I graduated. I turned my back for good on getting an education.

Second, I noticed great changes in my friends on the streets. During the year I was away many of the guys, and even the girls, had started mainlining heroin. While I had been getting my kicks out of booze and an occasional snort of heroin at Rockland, they had plunged deeper and deeper into the drug scene. They all looked awful, really down and out, with the greasy look of an addict who is past caring about his appearance. No one seemed to know how to have fun any more. No one wanted to party it up or go boozing. They were having babies and working angles to support their habits. Life outside the walls of Rockland sure looked less appealing close up.

By comparison, life in the Bronx didn't seem too bad. Getting away from the old scene might have been a good idea after all. Nina found herself a job in the restaurant part of a Spanish-American bar and managed to talk her employers into hiring me as a barmaid. What a great job for me! With my own enormous thirst and my love of night life, I was a natural for this line of work. No one seemed concerned that I was still a minor. I joked with the customers, mostly men, and matched the best of them in drinking beer. By midnight I was always smashed. Life didn't seem so bad when it could be kept at a distance with alcohol.

But soon I was feeling restless and angry again. I could almost understand why the gang had gotten into drugs: it was to combat the nothingness of this existence. Life still centered around crowded, dirty apartments with few luxuries. There was no real pleasure in living; there were no goals ahead. What we seemed to look forward to was just more of the same grinding poverty—for a lifetime.

Then Angelo came on the scene. A friend of one of my cousins, he was the first decent-looking fellow I'd seen in months. Compared to the sloppy junkies, he looked better than he should have. At least he was clean and wore clothes that showed he cared how he looked.

Since I had never been boy-crazy like some of the other debs back in the gang days, I was still a bit of a novice in relationships with men. In fact, except for the unhappy accident with Miguel, I'd had no sexual experience at all. I'd never "slept around" as many gang debs did. I really seemed to have no natural affection for men. They were just one more fact of life that had to be tolerated; and so far I had managed to tolerate them from a distance.

But Angelo appeared at a time when I was really bored with life. A prisoner of an existence which had no highs and lows, only suffocating sameness, I was beginning to despair of ever feeling any emotion again. I knew I'd lost a lot of my humanity at Rockland. I was beginning to fear they'd driven out *all* my emotions. I became desperate to feel something for someone. So I made Angelo my test case. I tried hard to feel something for him.

At first I didn't tell Angelo about my past—about the Diamonds and Rockland. If he thought he'd found a nice girl, different from the others, I sure wasn't telling him he was wrong. However, Angelo and I occasionally got drunk or smoked some pot together. At one of those times, in an unexpected attack of honesty, I told Angelo all about my past. He was furious! The nice girl he thought he'd found turned out to be like all the others, only luckier so far.

It took me a while to catch on to the fact that he was mostly enraged with *himself*. He thought *he* had been the clever one to hide his past from me. It seems that while I was locked up in Rockland, my friend Angelo had been doing time in jail. He had a past that included everything from armed robbery to heroin addiction and pushing heroin and other drugs. He had been clean when we first met only because he

58

too had been *kept* clean by barred doors. The game of pretending was over. We could finally get on with sharing the only thing we really had in common in the first place: our desire to escape the ugliness of the life around us.

Within four months of my release from Rockland, I was again snorting heroin—this time with Angelo for company. Then I discovered that it was taking too long to get high that way, and the effects wore off too quickly. So Angelo took care of getting me the works we needed to begin "skin popping"—injecting heroin into a muscle for a quicker high. That *was* a great improvement. Angelo was useful after all; I began to appreciate his experience and know-how. But I had taken about only eight doses of heroin by skin popping before I found that I needed even more of a high than I was getting by this route. A three-dollar bag of heroin simply disappeared in no time, and the high I got from it wasn't nearly high enough.

Angelo had already begun to mainline again and was only too glad to help me out. From the moment the first warm pleasure of an instant high hit my bloodstream from a needle plunged into my bulging vein, I was as good as addicted. I no longer needed any excuse to get high. Existing was excuse enough. My life of dependency on heroin had begun. I too was a junkie.

Only a short time later, I discovered I was pregnant. I was far from thrilled, but it was all right. Maybe a kid would settle me down and make me expect less out of living. It certainly seemed to work for other girls.

I was 17½ years old by then. Half-heartedly I asked Nina if she would sign a consent for us to be married—but I was neither surprised nor disappointed when she refused. To her it was a sin to marry a man you didn't love and would not stay with forever. Better just to live with him, have the baby, and see what happened. I knew she was right in my case, so I didn't fight it. I had no more affection for Angelo than I did for anyone else. I'd have his kid, but there was no sense making a big deal out of it.

I was aware that the baby I was carrying wasn't benefiting from my addiction, but I didn't think about it any more than necessary. In the fifth month of my pregnancy, however, my maternal instinct struggled to the fore, and I decided to have a go at my first "cure," to get clean for the baby.

At that time the city of New York was offering a "twenty-one-day cure" that consisted of daily decreasing doses of an early form of methadone. I stayed with the treatment only two weeks. It was *hopeless!* Oh, I was getting rid of the physiological craving all right, but there was no effective treatment for the mind habit. I *wanted* to be high, because the life I led seemed too miserable to be endured otherwise. No one could change those circumstances of life. No one could change *me.* Hooked or clean, I was still an ex-gang deb, pregnant by a guy I didn't much like, let alone *love,* a drunkard, a pothead, and finally a *junkie!* Those facts of life could not be faced without help. Heroin helped!

On July 31, my son was born in the Bronx Lebanon Hospital. He arrived almost two months ahead of schedule, as is frequently the case with the offspring of junkies. Since he weighed only three pounds, he required many weeks in a hospital incubator to catch up. I never learned if he had been born addicted.

In any case, it was not Angelo I was so happy to see during hospital visiting hours. By early evening on the day of delivery my stitches were becoming rather painful, and the white powder he brought with him was just what I needed. I celebrated Dondi's arrival by getting high on junk the evening of his birth.

Chapter 9

A WAY OF LIFE

Junkies don't make good mothers. The children of junkies always have a rival for their parents' affections. This rival is evil and more powerful than the strongest mother love. A junkie's need for a fix always seems greater and more compelling to her than any need her child might have.

Dondi was lucky to have Nina. She should not have had to take on yet another child to raise, especially in view of the heartbreak she had suffered from her attempts to raise my mother and me. But she knew, and so did I, that I would be incompetent as a mother. She accepted the full responsibility for Dondi's care. When he finally came home to Nina's apartment after his extended stay in the hospital nursery, I was nothing more than an occasional visitor there.

For a few more months Angelo and I continued to live together off and on, but our relationship became very tiresome. There just wasn't any love in me to give—to anyone.

Then my drug habit really began to catch up with me. When I first started mainlining a small bag of heroin lasted all day, enabling me to work at various jobs to support my habit. I would need a fix by the end of the workday, but I could usually function satisfactorily while on the job. During this time I worked sporadically in the garment district, where the pay for a steampresser was enough for my initial drug needs.

Once I landed a job at one of the finest department stores, first in the gift-wrapping department at Christmas, then in the stock room, and finally in the knitwear department. The buyer in this last department took a special interest in me and had plans to train me as her assistant. But by then my five-dollar-a-day habit had grown to a twenty-dollar habit. In spite of the promise of better pay to come, it was quite literally impossible for me to wait. I began shoplifting to supplement my income, and was shortly thereafter caught and fired by the department store management.

Eventually, like most other junkies, I had to depend chiefly on stealing to cover my growing drug expenses. Since shoplifted items could seldom be resold at their original prices, I often had to steal twice the amount in merchandise to realize enough in cash to pay for my drugs. Working this angle soon became really big business.

Along with other junkies, I often took actual shopping orders from neighborhood families. I'd take their money, pocket it, and go to the supermarkets and steal what they desired—a chicken here, a loaf of bread there. Although I became very adept, almost professional, in such "shopping" techniques, the possibility of getting caught and busted by the police was still a very real one. Nevertheless, shoplifting remained the easiest way for me to earn the money I needed to keep myself supplied with enough junk to satisfy my body's ever-increasing appetite.

I never stopped to consider the "right" or "wrong" of this activity. I needed money, and shoplifting gave me what I needed. Morality was dictated by necessity—the necessity of feeding my drug habit.

As I was acquiring this new morality and learning all the angles of my new business, I also acquired a new name. "Cookie" was just the first of many aliases I used in various parts of the city as I pursued a life of crime full time. I was Naomi and Esther in other areas; but in the Bronx, where I first began "working the angles," I was called Cookie. Cookie became the nickname that stuck. Eventually the name Cookie Rivera became rather notorious in police circles. But that was not until some time later.

Eventually I also stole from my family. At first I'd just drop by Nina's and pick up whatever I needed. I felt that many of her possessions were really mine anyway. After all, hadn't I shared the booty of some really big heists with her and Dondi? Once, I was really desperate for a fix and too sick from withdrawal to go downtown to "shop" in the usual manner. Thoughts of Nina's apartment full of furniture came to mind. With the help of a cousin who had a truck, I unloaded everything in her apartment—the television set and all the furniture except for one small bed—and sold them for $300. Few of those possessions had been paid for by Nina, who like almost everyone on welfare found buying "on time" a way of life. But I felt I needed a fix worse than my grandmother and my small son needed chairs to sit on.

I was wise enough to stay away from Nina's for several weeks after that. When I finally did return to visit, I found that my welcome had worn a bit thin.

"Irmita, you bum! What makes you such a liar and a thief? You hooked on junk like all your friends?" Nina practically spat out each word as she spoke.

Until this time my grandmother had always believed me when I denied that I was a junkie. The other members of my family—uncles and aunts—tried to tell her, but she remained defensive of her Irmita. This time I rolled up my sleeves to show her the "railroad tracks," those telltale needle marks progressing up my arm. "This answer your question, Nina?" I sneered.

"You get out! We don't need junkies here. Don't come to Nina for money for your fixes. You stay away, hear me? We don't want you here!"

I went. She had nothing left for me to steal anyway, and I surely did not want to hear her lectures on drugs. I knew them by heart. No junkie that I knew of was ever helped by lectures. And I felt sure I knew what I was doing. I could take care of myself.

I *did* take care of myself—at least fairly well—until the first heroin shortage. In 1960 the authorities were successful in closing down a large heroin supplier for the city of New York. For a time heroin was hard to get and very expensive. A trey, the three-dollar bag of heroin, jumped to three and four times the normal price. Instead of costing me $20 to $40 a day, my habit suddenly cost a whopping $60 to $120—that is, when I could find someone to sell me the stuff. Withdrawal sickness became a recurring nightmare.

"Oh, man, am I ever hurtin'! I don't think I can take any more of this. I just gotta have a fix!" These thoughts were interrupted by yet another spasm of knifing abdominal pain followed by violent, heaving nausea. My stomach, long emptied, held nothing left to vomit, but still the wrenching spasms came—

"OK, Cookie, *think!* Where can you get some money? You've got to get a fix before you're too weak to find any. And I'll just bet there isn't any to be found in the whole damn city!"

I'd been pondering my dilemma for hours before the realization hit me that I was finally desperate enough to sell myself for a fix. Up until this time, going out into the streets to "turn a trick" (solicit a guy for paid sex) had been too repulsive to me to consider seriously. For a female junkie, especially a young one like me, prostitution was the most reliable way to keep up with the growing expenses of a drug habit. Many of my friends already supported themselves and a fellow with their street earnings. In exchange for financial support, their old man offered them at least minimal protection from the perverts who roamed the streets in search of a girl to abuse.

The thought was slow to come to mind, but suddenly it was full-blown. "You want fast money? You know what you gotta do. Get out there and turn a quick trick before you are too sick to walk!

"No, I just can't! I don't want any stinkin' man messin' around with me! I *can't!*" It took quite a while before this personal revulsion was overruled by my body's desperate physiological demands. I could not stand the idea of prostitution; but neither could I tolerate the physical torture I was enduring. I needed a *fix!* So I called a relative of mine who had a friend—

It was the fastest money I'd ever made. Fifty dollars for a man to take whatever pleasure he could from my unwilling body. No wonder so many girls ended up prostituting for their money. Incredible as it seemed, a girl could always find someone willing to pay for sex, no matter how drug-ridden and shopworn the wares.

I insisted that I was somehow different from all the rest. "This kind of life is not for *me,* thank you. The money is fine, but the job stinks! I've got too much pride for that. Cookie Rivera isn't any whore!" Such ideas might return briefly, when I was feeling reassured by the old familiar warmth in my veins. But when the first waves of nausea and the cold perspiring would start, I would begin the argument all over again. I hated myself for giving in, but heroin couldn't be bought with lofty ideals. I was too well hooked to be able to resist such a readily available source of income.

However, I did not develop a feeling that prostituting was a permanent way of life. I was just making do until this crisis passed. I never got myself an old man to support, and I never thought about the next trick. Each time, I'd wait until the situation was getting desperate before I'd go back into the streets. Despite the fact that it was easier to pick someone up when you were high, and much easier to tolerate what followed, I always waited. I was so sure that *this* time it would not be necessary. Something else would turn up if I could just wait a little longer.

Nothing but more stealing and more prostitution ever turned up to earn me what I needed to exist. What began in desperation did indeed become a way of life.

Chapter 10

THE "CURES"

During a drug shortage there are times when a junkie cannot find a fix at *any* price. Despite my new source of income, there were occasions when the drug I needed simply could not be purchased. At such times I thought a bit more seriously about the possible alternatives to my addiction. At first I didn't think in terms of a permanent cure for my habit. I just wanted to get temporarily free enough to make it through a shortage—then start again with a decreased heroin requirement at a lower daily cost. The idea of getting completely free seemed both impossible and unappealing. I still wanted the drug. I just did not like the way I had to scramble to *get* the stuff. Heroin was all the more necessary to me at this point because I needed to forget *more;* I had to forget how I'd been earning the money to support my habit. This vicious cycle of my existence rolled on. I felt that it could possibly be slowed down from time to time, but certainly not halted.

Voluntary admissions to the state hospital became very popular among addicts during heroin shortages. I took these "ninety-day cures" more than once. Checking into Rockland, I'd be assigned to ward 10, the medical ward. Once dried out, I'd be released to start over again. This short-term therapy provided the medical help I needed while kicking, but did very little to break the psychological habit. The psychiatrists really did try to help me, but I still *wanted* to take heroin long after my body ceased craving it. Life and all its ugliness remained unchanged. So I still needed to escape from it somehow.

Nevertheless these "cures" helped some by cutting down on the size of the dose I needed to get a satisfactory high. I had learned that occasionally getting clean was essential to staying alive. Without some time spent off the drug, whether in a hospital or in a jail, the average junkie would be dead within a year or two from disease, malnutrition, impure drugs, or an overdose. A junkie does not take care of himself when left alone. I was no exception. The trips to Rockland helped me stay alive.

During one of my voluntary confinements in Rockland, a female psychiatrist tried to help me. She felt that the "mind habit" of a junkie was mainly one of a failure of willpower. She tried to assure me over and over, "Cookie, I *know* you've got the willpower to lick this thing. You don't really want to die a miserable junkie; you're too smart for that. You just need to prove to yourself that you've got the willpower."

She seemed so *sure*, so confident that I was smarter and stronger than the other junkies! Someone with confidence in me was a rare specimen by then. How was I to go about seeing if she was right?

Her remedy was succinct: "Kick 'cold turkey'!"

"Cold turkey? Hey, man, I've done that *lots* of times. How do you think I kicked in jail? Or when there is no stuff around?" The idea seemed pretty dumb to me.

"No, Cookie. I'm not talking about kicking like that when you don't have any choice. I mean *choosing* to do it. Voluntarily declining to take drugs when they are available will do it for you, prove your willpower. If you can do *that*, you'll be cured."

"You mean you want me to sit in a room and be sick like that with the stuff right outside in the street waiting for me? I can't do it!"

"But I know you *can* if you really want to get cured," the psychiatrist continued to argue. "Just think—no more selling yourself. You could be *really* free. You've got the willpower, if you want to try. I *know* this would work for you."

She was so *sure* she had hit upon the answer for me that her confidence was contagious. By the time we had talked Nina into letting me come to her place to try this noble experiment, I felt that I was Supergirl.

Somehow I *did* it! Three days of pure hell passed before the withdrawal symptoms subsided and I felt that I just *might* live. I had kicked cold turkey voluntarily. Drugs were right outside the door, but I *did* it.

I was weak from the violent vomiting and unrelenting pain of withdrawal and hungry from involuntary fasting, but I really felt strong inside. That lady psychiatrist had been right about me. I was something else!

The day I realized I'd made it, I struggled out of bed for the first time and wobbled over to the dresser. I looked like hell but could not refrain from grinning at the girl who stared at me from the mirror. "Hi there. Cookie Rivera—girl wonder! You are really fantastic! Kicking drugs right in the old neighborhood. How does it feel to be so strong?"

It felt *great!* I was giddy with success. It had been so long since I had a reason to feel proud of myself!

I made an attempt to tidy up and put on a blouse and slacks, the best I owned, to rejoin Nina and

Dondi in the world outside that room. Nina was as delighted as I. Hope had been rekindled in those tired, wary eyes of hers, and now she could not contain her pleasure. She patted my arm, stroked my hair, and wept. "How long have I prayed for this day? How long have I waited to get you back, Irmita? I am so happy! I am so proud!"

It had been a long time since Nina had shown affection for me. Not since I'd joined the gang had she expressed outright approval of what I did. Emotions long buried deep within began to struggle to the surface.

This rare surge of sentiment spilled over to my son. Dondi hardly knew me, I'd been so small a part of his young life. But I knew suddenly that I really did love him. I tried to hold and fondle him, but he tolerated my clumsy efforts only briefly before tearing himself away to rejoin his beloved Nina. Such unsought affection was too much for him to take from this stranger who was his mother.

As the news of my successful cold-turkey withdrawal gradually spread through the tenement grapevine, neighbors and relatives began to drop by to see for themselves. Their congratulations held a "we'll have to wait and see" tone that made me furious. Who were they to stand there gawking at me like I was some kind of freak in a sideshow and making all their jokes about junkies? What did they know about real willpower? I'd *done* it! I was free now. I wasn't some freak; I was *normal*.

Nina's eyes followed my every move. She sensed my changing mood and watched apprehensively as I began to pace the apartment like a caged animal. When I casually remarked that I was going to "step outside for a breath of fresh air," she was at my side at once pleading, "Don't *do* it! Stay inside. You're not *ready*. You've got to get stronger before you go out there. They'll just sell you more dope."

Her concern, justified though it was, caused all the old rebellion to well up within me. My system was clean of heroin, but not of hatred and hostility. I had not been given any new resources for handling anger and frustration. I could only see that Nina did not trust me, that she was trying to tell me what to do. It made me mad.

"Look, I know what I'm doing!" I shouted. "I'm cured. I did it cold turkey, didn't I? I've just got to get away from all these people, that's all. They're enough to make me *want* a fix! I'll be fine if you will just leave me alone!"

As I slammed the door, I caught the amused "I told you so" expression my uncle was giving my aunt with a wink and a nudge.

In the five blocks that separated Nina's place from my favorite haunt, the bar, I managed to cool off a little. After all, what did my family know? I was the expert on drug addiction, and I had done the impossible. I paused only a second before entering the bar—long enough to remind myself of the willpower I possessed.

"Cookie! We heard you was tryin' to kick. That's a real bummer! Glad to see it's not true. Welcome back!"

"Welcome back?" Welcome back to the darkness of a world where willpower is no power at all. Within two hours I had bought a bag of heroin and was flying as high as ever.

I never intended to try for a real cure after that. But continued sporadic shortages of heroin forced me to try a "therapeutic community." The psychiatrists felt that they had come up with a different approach to the problem, and thought I ought to give them a try. Why not? I was sure getting tired of those trips to Rockland.

The therapeutic community certainly did have a different approach. Rather than trying to bolster my self-image as the psychiatrists did, community therapists used methods that aimed at destroying the ego. During a therapy session they put me in the center of a circle and told me I was a "no-good, dirty dope addict"—real news to me, of course! The language they used was street language, coarse and ugly, and they shouted and jeered at me as they talked. The object was to get me angry enough to fight back. I naturally obliged. After half an hour of arguing with all of them at one time, however, I was so exhausted that I'd agree with everything they said. "Yes, I'm no good. Yes, you're right, I'm not worth anything."

And that is as far as the therapeutic community took me—right back where I started. I already knew I was a no-good junkie. I had been looking for a way to change that. Like all the other cures, the therapeutic community did not offer any way to alter *me*. And I was still a no-good junkie.

Finding no help from psychiatry and psychology, I turned to spiritualism. While Catholicism is the national religion of Puerto Rico, spiritualism is regarded by the people as the source of real spiritual power.

I was no stranger to *las veladas*, the séance-like meetings held by spiritualists. I had attended many back in Puerto Rico where my aunt had been a medium and the man next door was the "president of the table." I knew that spiritualists are supposed to be in touch with the spirits of the dead. They blame angry spirits for everything bad that happens, and all their medicine is aimed at protecting the individual from the curses of these spirits. I held no real belief in spiritualism but I certainly had felt accursed in my life. So, when I was fishing around for answers to my problems, I sought the advice of spiritualists in New York City.

I did not think much of their idea of curing my addiction by bathing in their foul-smelling potions—but one of their beliefs caught my interest. This was that, because my father had committed suicide, his spirit was unable to rest. They believed that he was trying to get my attention by putting a curse on me. If I could get in touch with him, he could tell me what I needed to do to help him find rest. Despite my skepticism, I went to several veladas in the hope that one day his spirit would show up.

One night it seemed that his spirit did appear. The velada was barely under way when the president of the table came over to me and jumped me. His fingers closed around my throat and began to tighten. He might well have succeeded in choking the life out of me, such was the supernatural strength of his trance, but several men pulled him off and tied him down until he revived.

My father's spirit seemed to have a dangerous way of communicating with me. I suddenly lost all desire to talk to *him*. If he had indeed put the curse on me that made me a drug addict, then I would just have to die a drug addict. It was obvious that he had not changed his mind about me.

Once all these routes for help had been traveled without success, I was more certain than ever that no cure existed for me. The best I could expect was the temporary relief afforded by a short stay in the hospital when I got too "strung out" from excessive drug dosage. All that seemed to remain in life for me was a slow death on drugs or a quick violent one in the streets.

Chapter 11

IN THE STREETS

Life out in the streets for the female addict is hazardous in the extreme. I had discovered this when I first began prostituting and a fellow addict tried to "take me off" (rob me) for his own fix. Junkies form a subculture, a family of sorts, with certain rules of mutual cooperation. But within the family are plenty of members who don't think twice about abusing the weakest members for their own fix. Female addicts are most often the weakest. I was never safe—even from my own kind.

Ralphie was one of those addicts who chose to live off the others by force. If you had money for a fix, you avoided Ralphie at all costs.

I had nothing on me and was sick with withdrawal the day he accosted me; so I did not feel the fear I should have.

"Cookie, go get my works for me. There are cops over there and I need a fix," was his opener.

It was not at all unusual for a fellow to ask a girl to obtain and carry his syringe, needle and other equipment, or "works," when the police were around. They would frisk a guy thoroughly at the drop of a hat but searching a girl is against New York City law, unless done by a policewoman. I was so weak and sick, I foolishly protested, "Aw, come on, Ralphie. Give me a break! I'm too sick, man!"

A huge hand clamped on my arm and I was dragged to a doorway. "I said, get in there and get my works!"

"OK, OK, Ralphie. Sure, man. I'll get your stuff for you, but I really *am* sick. You're all heart!" I tried to keep my tone light and sarcastic, but fear was beginning to grow. Ralphie could be really ugly when crossed.

"Up the steps—it's up there!" Now his orders were hissed rather than shouted.

On legs that shook from weakness, I stumbled up the stairs of the abandoned building, and realized that he was sending me to the roof six floors up.

"I thought you wanted your works, Ralphie. What's up here? Ralphie?"

His big fist hit me right in the face and I fell in my tracks. Whether it was because I had resisted him when he first asked me to get his works, or whether he was just in the mood for a little sick fun, I never knew. But the next four hours were a nightmare of beatings, sexual abuse, and threats of being thrown off the roof of that old building. By the time he was through, I was so ill from withdrawal and abuse I felt I would surely die. But uppermost in my mind, and ranking in importance even ahead of getting a fix, was the burning desire to kill Ralphie. Some day, somehow, I would have to find a way to put him away for good.

I survived this experience to find that there were other torturers around to prey upon physical frailty. Being particularly small in stature, I had only my wits to protect me from such men—and in times of desperation my wits were often beclouded by junk or by my needs for junk. I had my personal encounters with sadists, but nothing fed my fears quite the way Rosa's did.

77

I had been standing on the street talking with Rosa one morning before both of us turned our first trick of the day. An old-timer, she was looking pretty strung out again. Our nickname for her was *La Piojosa* ("Lice"), because she had plenty. Suddenly I felt hungry and decided to find some food before getting down to business. As I walked away, I looked back over my shoulder and saw Rosa getting into a light green sedan. "Ah, Rosa's got her first business," I thought to myself as I turned into a bar.

Two weeks later Rosa's dismembered parts were found in various places in Central Park, identifiable only from fingerprints. Rosa's last "trick" had been a maniac. It appeared that I had been the last person to see her alive, and I was questioned repeatedly by the police in their attempt to gain some clue to the killer's identity.

"You know it could easily have been you, don't you, Cookie?" was the way the detective put it.

Man! Did I ever think about *that!* If I had stayed on the corner with Rosa, the chances are excellent that I would have been the one the killer took into the car with him. I was no bargain, but I was younger and cleaner than La Piojosa. From that moment on, my fears while on the streets multiplied. I had to overcome not only self-loathing and disgust with the business of prostituting, but also the paralyzing fear of being brutally tortured and murdered like Rosa. No wonder my drug requirement was soaring! I had more and more to forget. Would this nightmare of life never end?

No, the nightmare was endless. There were always new variations of pain to endure, new ways to die a little at a time, especially if you were a female addict. One way was in Prostitute Court.

Like all the street girls, I had been picked up more

than once for loitering with intent to solicit. After a night in jail, they usually let me go for lack of proof of any actual wrongdoing. When you got as far as Prostitute Court, it was because they really had evidence to present.

For some reason, being taken to this court had a particularly dehumanizing effect on me. Like animals, we were all herded together and given the legally required blood test for venereal disease. Then we were examined very thoroughly by doctors and nurses. In our number would be some high-class call girls in mink who invariably got nicer treatment. Money still seemed to buy better breaks.

What really got to me was the moment when I was taken before the judge to hear the detective describe what he had seen me doing. Usually I was already sick with withdrawal symptoms. Hearing my "two-minute job"—which I managed to think of as only a business—described in four-letter words and graphic detail by a blunt detective, who had spied on the whole process, made me sicker yet.

No matter how low I felt, no matter how much self-contempt I had when I was dragged into Prostitute Court, I always felt lower and more contemptible when I came out. Whether I was sentenced to ninety days in jail, put into a hospital ward, or paroled, I lost more of myself every time I had to endure those proceedings.

Clearly a girl out in the streets was separated from normal life in a variety of ways that even a male addict could not understand. She was at the very bottom of the totem pole of respectability. What she did to exist robbed her of herself. Most people who'd been around the drug scene very long were convinced that rehabilitation of the female addict was impossible because of what she had to do out in the world of drugs.

At nineteen, I was as lacking in hope as any. I spent my days working angles to buy drugs, taking drugs to escape life, sleeping off the drugs I had taken, or suffering withdrawal pain and the ever-present fears that tortured a drug-free mind. Life was living hell. Surely I had hit rock bottom by now!

Chapter 12

A BAD TRIP

I stumbled up the stairs from the dirty basement of the tenement, blinking in surprise to find that it was already morning. The dark interior of the "shooting gallery" below, where I had gone the night before to take my fix, gave no clue to the time of day. How many hours had it been? Had I used up those precious few hours of my high just sleeping it off? What a waste! Now I'd just have to start all over again.

Already the cold sweat was forming on my forehead. Before I turned any tricks today, I'd need a fix. Where was Neno or Danny? I'd also need a crime partner if I had to take someone off for some money. Even with my trusty knife in hand, a girl my size could not expect to pull off a job like that alone. Certainly I couldn't when I needed a fix! Dammit! Weren't any of the fellows around? If I had the stuff already, they sure wouldn't be so hard to find. Where *was* everyone?

When eventually I found my fellow addicts in a nearby bar, I heard the chilling news in disbelief. Another heroin panic was upon us. The stuff had disappeared overnight. The last three-dollar bag that anyone had seen had been sold for fifty dollars. By morning there were no bags to be found at any price. How could it happen so fast? A junkie had no warning at all. Man, it was gonna be a lousy day!

The panic of 1961 made all the other shortages insignificant by comparison. Heroin had just disappeared for the junkie in the street. Everywhere there were weak, wretching shadows desperately searching for a fix. Hospital emergency rooms were crammed with junkies seeking relief from the sickness. And the waiting line for admission to Rockland was suddenly a mile long. In sheer desperation junkies started shooting anything and everything into their veins. Even aspirin was tried. Then *bombitas*, the forerunner of "speed," suddenly came into their own.

I was as desperate as the others. So I took bombitas too, even though I knew they were very unpredictable. Life was always unpredictable, and at that point it was also intolerable.

One trouble with the high from bombitas was that you never got to sleep. On heroin you slept as you came down, and held off withdrawal symptoms a little longer. On bombitas, sleep was impossible and withdrawal was sheer torture.

I had been taking bombitas around the clock for several days when I started seeing the "baby cops." Those infants in the baby carriages or strollers *looked* like babies all right, but I was certain they were actually policemen spying on me. I tried to warn the other junkies, but they only laughed and started looking at me strangely. I was afraid to trust anyone. No one seemed to understand the danger but me.

Somehow I found myself at Nina's. Had I traveled there alone, or had someone taken me?

"Irmita, sit down. You'll be OK." That must be Nina. "Nina! Help me get these bugs off of me! I hate those ugly crawling things!"

"What bugs, Irmita? There aren't any bugs!"

82

Stupid old Nina! Too blind to see the ugly black bugs that had started to swarm over my arms and legs. "Get 'em off! Get 'em off!"

Then I awakened in a darkened room. Now how did I get in bed? While I was struggling to remember, a sudden thought seized me: "That man I killed! Oh, God, the blood! It's still all over my knife and my hands. Gotta wash the blood off!"

I nearly knocked Nina over trying to get to the sink. "Oh, Nina, I'm sorry—so sorry! I didn't mean to kill him. Gotta get this blood off!"

Nina's eyes were widened with fear as she half-whispered, "There's no blood, Irmita. You are sick—crazy maybe. You are seeing things."

But then I heard the police pounding on the door. Clutching my knife, I ran to the window. The street was nearly empty of traffic in the early morning hours, but dozens of police cars surrounded the place. Well, they wouldn't find me easy to take. I still had my knife with me.

In sheer panic Nina had run to a neighbor's apartment and phoned my uncle for help. My ravings had scared her to death. There were no bugs; there had been no murder; there were no police outside to get me. The other bad effect of bombitas had caught up with me. My mind was a battlefield between genuine perception and hallucination.

My uncle managed to get me as far as Bellevue and eventually I was admitted to Rockland again. This time I was no addict getting dried out on the medical ward. I was now a real mental case. In my rare lucid moments, I knew enough to be scared. "You'll be locked up for good now," I told myself at such times. "You've cooked your brain for good. Can't make sense out of anything." My panic grew.

I was back on ward 21. The violent ward was a little hard to recognize in my twisted state. I was hard to recognize too. Dr. Philips did not know the miserable wretch I had become. He remembered the sassy, tough gang deb he had treated five years before. This creature was a filthy, deranged junkie and prostitute. Disgust should have made him turn his back on me, but still he wanted to help.

When, after two months, my mind seemed to come around again, Dr. Philips was the one I went to for help. "How long does a mother have to go before she gets to see her little boy?" I whined. "And how come I never got a pass, as long as I've been comin' here?"

I had not lost my ability to work any angle for my own selfish ends. I really did not particularly care about seeing Dondi, but I was not above using him to my advantage.

Dr. Philips was as kind as ever. He got me a pass and called Nina to tell her to bring Dondi in for a visit that Sunday.

The day was beautiful. I was outside the gates visiting with Dondi while Nina was in Dr. Philips' office discussing my progress. Suddenly the ease of just walking away was too tempting to resist. I took my 2½-year-old son, walked to a bus, and headed back to New York City.

When I was discovered missing, a thirteen-state alarm went out. Although I was Dondi's mother, I was not his legal guardian; Nina was. I was wanted for kidnapping. Realizing that it was Dondi they were really concerned about, I left him in the lobby of an aunt's apartment house, phoned my aunt to tell her where to pick him up, and congratulated myself for understanding my grandmother so well.

84

A few months later I dropped in to see her and Dondi. But the last ounce of Nina's sympathy for me had been exhausted by my latest betrayal. She and my uncle quickly turned me over to the authorities, and I soon found myself on my way back to Rockland. Nina too had given up on me.

This time I was sent straight to building 60, the "Snake Pit," where the hopelessly insane were kept. I'd lost my last friend at Rockland when I ran out on Dr. Philips. There would be no more chances to betray trust and work angles. There were no angles to work in building 60.

Most of the patients in the Snake Pit had been there ten or fifteen years already. Old wrecks of humanity, they were the most repulsive creatures I'd ever seen. One woman who walked in tiny circles all the time so annoyed me that I'd often push her down or trip her to stop her walking. One day she dropped dead right in front of all of us.

The windows were too high to see out of and visitors were strictly limited to one every two or three months. It was almost a year before I had any visitors! Then Nina relented and came to see me. When she saw the conditions of my existence, she broke into tears. Then she went right out and hired a lawyer. Once more she was my ally.

The lawyer offered the hospital my deportation in exchange for my release. Since this meant one less hopeless case for tax dollars to support, the hospital board agreed. I was taken directly to the airport and placed aboard a plane bound for Puerto Rico. A minimum of two years would have to pass before I could return to the States.

Nina had allowed me to take Dondi with me in the hope that somehow he would help to settle me down.

Two weeks later Dondi and I returned to Nina's apartment in New York. An assumed name was really no trouble for a junkie used to working the angles.

Chapter 13

SOMEBODY UP THERE

Even this miraculous reprieve from a lifetime in the Snake Pit did not suffice to change my way of living. I knew only one way to exist. I returned to the streets—to the shooting galleries, the two-minute tricks for money, the stealing and burglary with one crime partner or another. I was an old-timer who knew every angle in the book.

It was tricks I was looking for, not trouble, when the tall, husky guy came up and grabbed me. I was so high on all the drugs I was taking that I'm not sure I recognized he was a policeman until he said, "Looking for a little business, are you, sister? Well, not today. You're coming with me!"

I still could not stand being pushed around. I pulled my knife on him and started to fight back. I guess I bloodied him a bit (they told me his face required several stitches) but I remembered nothing. In jail I soon learned all the details. According to the paper, a girl five feet tall had beaten up a six-foot policeman. That wasn't quite accurate, because I had been beaten up pretty badly too. The policemen who responded to their buddy's call for assistance had seen his facial injury and had subdued me by a beating so severe that my leg was broken in the process. I had been booked for felonious assualt on a policeman.

"You can plead guilty and get a 'light' sentence of

twenty years," the court-appointed attorney told me, "or you can fight it and get longer. They'll get you one way or another, Cookie. You just weren't very smart to cut a cop."

I decided to plead guilty. While I was waiting for my trial I got into another senseless fight in the prison dining room, and they put me in solitary confinement for inciting a riot in jail. That pretty well guaranteed that I would have to do those twenty years.

After many days in solitary, I was allowed to have a visitor—my lawyer. When he told me the authorities had decided to drop my case, I was first incredulous, then weak with relief. "What *happened?*" I asked him. "I thought they had me iced away for life."

"Well, Cookie, all I can say is that Somebody Up There must be watching over you. The police surgeons took pictures of your injuries the day you were brought in. It doesn't look good to a jury to see a ninety pound girl beaten to a pulp by six burly cops. They're afraid you'll turn the tables on them and sue the city. So they are going to let you go instead of taking a chance on bad publicity. You are really one lucky girl!"

Lucky maybe—but the "Man Upstairs" who was supposed to be pulling all the strings neglected to take care of the harassment I was subjected to from then on by all of New York City's Finest. Every cop on the beat knew Cookie Rivera then and took every opportunity to bust me for something after that. It was one junkie against the entire police force. Fame certainly had its disadvantages.

Still my life did not change much. Twice I had been miraculously saved from lengthy imprisonment. But I went right back to the same old way of living.

On the day of my near-fatal overdose, Manuel and

I had worked together to roll a drunk down in Little Korea and then take off a prostitute and her trick as she was finishing up business. It had been a good haul, and we were well supplied when we headed into the condemned building to take our fix. We'd avoided the usual shooting galleries for fear of having to share our wealth. So we were quite alone in that old basement—except for the rats.

Maybe it was the barbiturates I'd been taking all day, maybe I just got hold of some bad stuff. But that fix sure packed a mean wallop! Most overdoses kill within an hour. Yet seven hours passed before I was declared DOA in the emergency room and my family was called in to view the remains. Only Nina's hysterical refusal to accept my death saved me from being taken to the morgue.

This was my third reprieve within a year—and this time it was a reprieve from death itself. It seems incredible that I could not see a promise in all these miracles of survival. Instead, I saw only a continuation of hell stretching before me.

Chapter 14

A NEW DRESS

About four months after my brush with death, I was annoyed to find myself being followed by a fellow addict by the name of "One-Eyed Dutch," who had acquired his colorful name from the time he tried to take off someone who happened to be carrying a metal-pointed umbrella. In the skirmish, he lost an eye. But when Dutch started following me, he was clean—and he was more excited about his way of kicking junk than the female psychiatrist had been about will-power. It seemed that a bunch of fellows were finding help getting off drugs at a place called Teen Challenge. One-Eyed Dutch was sure that even a girl could get clean there too.

Even a *girl?* With all she'd have to forget to stay clean? Forget it!

"Beat it, Dutch! I'm tired of talking cures. There are no cures for me. I'm gonna die just like I am—a junkie!"

But Dutch was not put off by such tactics. His fervor was unmatched by anything I'd ever seen. He really seemed to *care* about me. It had been a long time since anyone had gone out of his way for me. As Dutch spoke of love and the man Jesus, I had vague recollections of something from an earlier day.

Oh, yes! Nicky Cruz, a gang leader turned preacher, had once taken me into his home to care for me while I was down and out and trying to kick. He and his wife Gloria had shown that same kind of caring. They had prayed with me and taken me everywhere with them while I was kicking, even when they were invited out to dinner. Nothing had been too much for them as they tried to minister to my needs. I had been impressed by their love, but failed to recognize its Source. I thought perhaps it was because Nicky was a fellow countryman that he tried to help. I had cut out as soon as I was strong enough. And now, here was someone else saying that Jesus wanted me, wanted to give me the victory over heroin, wanted to give me a new life. Dutch wasn't from my country; he was black. It had been years since anyone had told me I was wanted by anyone, unless you count being wanted by the police. Being wanted by Jesus sounded crazy.

I gave up after a full day of Dutch's insistence. I was pretty strung out anyway. Time I was getting dried out a bit. Might as well get Dutch off my back and go to Teen Challenge to kick. I knew of worse places to do it, and I could no longer voluntarily admit myself to Rockland. So One-Eyed Dutch took me in a car driven by a couple he knew to 416 Clinton Avenue, the Brooklyn home of Teen Challenge. Today, Teen Challenge is famous because of *The Cross and the Switchblade*, which was written by its founder, Dave Wilkerson. But back then it wasn't so well known. I had never heard of it. I walked in knowing nothing of what to expect.

I had to be screened by those in charge: Dave Wilkerson's brother Don, two other ministers, and the Dean of Women, Ruth Cowgill. When they asked me questions about my life, I felt certain they would soon see that I could not be accepted. Then they got to questioning me about how I supported my habit. I became embarrassed, confused, and angry.

"That's none of your business, Mister!" I snapped at Don Wilkerson.

He was calm but firm in replying, "Young lady, if you are coming here with that kind of attitude, we don't want you!"

There it was! They didn't want to help the likes of me. This place was for *some* kids maybe, but I was different—a Spick, a junkie, a prostitute. This "love" thing was for people who were different from me.

I was quick to retort, "Mister, you can keep your Teen Challenge! I don't want *you* either!" I turned to leave. No one was going to say that Cookie Rivera had begged for help.

That should have ended my association with Teen Challenge right then and there. But something deep within me told me I was a fool, that these people *did* want to help me, if I'd let them.

It was really tough to apologize. A few seconds passed before I mustered enough courage to reverse my stand. "I didn't really mean what I said. I *do* want help. Please give me a break. Let me stay! You say Jesus can heal me. Then give me that chance."

I could see them waver, obviously sensing a challenge to their faith that Jesus could handle *every* problem, even one that looked as hopeless as I. Then it seemed that there wasn't an unoccupied bed in the place. I was sure I had just wasted that apology. But Ruth said, "Don, she can sleep in *my* bed!" And with that it was settled. I had gained a champion and was allowed to stay.

I had been high during that first interview, but not too high to hear them say I'd have to come off the stuff cold turkey. That didn't bother me too much at the time: I was too tired and high enough not to worry about what was to come. I was asleep before I felt the bed beneath me.

When I awoke the next morning, the idea of cold-turkey withdrawal didn't seem at all appealing. The last few times I had gone that route, I had ended up having convulsions and getting admitted to the hospital. Realizing what was coming, I knew it was time to get dressed and be ready to get on the street for a fix.

But my dirty blue jeans, torn shirt, and old jacket were gone. So was my knife! I muttered a few oaths before I saw what was there in their place. A new dress! Brand new! How long had it been since I'd had any new clothes? And it fit my bony, eighty-five-pound frame just right. When I put it on I could hardly believe the image in the mirror. "Not bad! Not bad at all!"

"Good morning, Cookie. Did you sleep well?" I whirled to face the broad smile of Ruth Cowgill. The love I had heard in her voice was quite visible now in her eyes. I was used to patronizing people who only *talked* about helping you. But this woman seemed genuine. I had no defenses prepared to handle the power of a love that expected nothing in return.

I could only stammer, "I—I *know* I'm gonna be sick!"

"No, you're not! We've been praying for you all night."

These people just had to be crazy or something! First this woman is willing to give up her own bed for me. Then they buy me a new dress for my filthy junkie body. And *then*, they pray to combat the withdrawal symptoms of heroin.

But the fact was obvious that I *wasn't* getting sick and vomiting in pain like I always did by this time in the streets. What kind of power did these prayers have? Was it possible that I had again fallen in with spiritualists?

My condition remained essentially unchanged all day. I was kicking, but I sure couldn't prove it. I went to lunch. Then I went to supper. No sickness! I couldn't believe it! And all around me were people who were praising Jesus and thanking Him for helping me. I didn't understand it at all, but I did know that some very real Power was at work in their love and concern: After all, I really *did* kick cold turkey without ever getting sick. How about that?

Chapter 15

PLEASE MAKE ME CRY

Not everything went as smoothly as kicking drugs. The memory of the Power that had released me from heroin kept me at Teen Challenge long after I stopped hoping that this Jesus business would ever work for me. It wasn't the discipline of the place—although there was plenty—that turned me off. I found it very easy to fit into a routine, to "play the game" according to the rules, except for the rule forbidding smoking. If I had been addicted to junk, I was even more addicted to cigarettes. I found it impossible to do without them. But all the other rules were nothing compared to Rockland or jail. I could stand the discipline all right.

It was just that everyone seemed so different from me. All the counselors were nice clean white folks, mostly from the Midwest. They had never lived in a ghetto except by choice, as they were doing now. I felt sure they could not possibly understand what it was to live in poverty so degrading that the misery of a junkie's life was preferable to enduring it. And they certainly couldn't know the self-loathing a girl can feel when she remembers how she had been earning her money. They were decent, whole, secure, and loving because they had *always* been decent, whole, secure, and loved. What they had was not possible for me.

Even the other junkies in the program seemed different. I was twenty-three years old—older than the other girls—and no one had as much to live down as I did. Actually, only the guys seemed to be really making it this way. I could understand that. *They* had never had to sell themselves to drugs. They had been just as hooked as I was; but when they got clean, they could go out into society and forget the past. A girl who had lost her respectability could never regain it. The prospect for such a girl to shake her past was mighty dim.

At first I cooperated to the extent of saying, "Jesus come into my heart," just as I was told to. Nothing happened. No new life fell upon me, no release of hatred. Nothing. I concluded that Jesus didn't work for female junkies.

From that point on, I became a real obstacle to the workers. I was just putting in time to get healthy, gain a little weight, and get back home on the streets again. I needled the other girls in the program and started fights. Once I tried to throw one of the girls down the stairs. Although she suffered no real injury, I expected to be kicked out. I expected it every time I was called on the carpet, and that was often. But no one told me I should go.

The chapel in the Clinton Avenue building was a plain, large room. We'd all sit on folding chairs as the guys in the program testified to their changed lives. They talked of being set free from drugs and from hatred. And they expressed sorrow for the lives they had led. *That* I couldn't understand. I had *never* felt sorry for the things I had done. I'd felt anger, hatred, and shame—but never sorrow. I did what I *had* to do to get by. The sight of those boys crying over what they'd done in the past embarrassed me. I *never*

cried! I didn't know how. I'd just snicker and jeer.
Genuine emotion was beyond me.

In spite of recognizing that the rehabilitation program was not reaching me, I stuck with it. I still have
no idea *why!* I know that Ruth Cowgill's faith in me
and the incredible patience of the whole staff really
helped. But still I stayed long beyond the time I had
planned, and much longer than the staff expected me
to. It was winter, and those streets were cold and
dreary. I was eating well and staying warm at Clinton Avenue. Why should I be in a hurry to move on?

Nevertheless, moving on was part of the rehabilitation plan. Once a girl had been at the center for a
few weeks and showed any inclination to stick with
the program, she was automatically moved to the
girls' residence in Rhinebeck, New York. I'd never
been anywhere in America outside of New York
City—except across the George Washington Bridge to
Rockland—until I was transferred to Rhinebeck.
Compared to the crowded ghettos of New York,
Rhinebeck was the end of the earth. The home was an
isolated, bleak-looking old mansion on the banks of
the Hudson River. I hated it there and decided that it
was soon going to be time to cut out.

Then I heard about the trip to Pittsburgh. Every
month Dave Wilkerson held a meeting at the Syria
Mosque in Pittsburgh where Kathryn Kuhlman held
her Miracle Services. In fact it was through the
friendship and invitation of Miss Kuhlman that he
was given the privilege of these meetings. This month
we were invited to go along for a big youth rally. All
of the girls at Rhinebeck and all the guys from the
Teen Challenge farm at Rehrersburg, Pennsylvania,
would be travelling by bus to Pittsburgh. That
sounded like a pretty good party to me. It would also
be my first chance to get outside the state of New

York. Yeah—that was worth hanging around for. There'd be plenty of time to split when we got back.

The big auditorium was jammed. There must have been a few thousand kids in that place. Even I found it hard not to be moved by the excitement of such a crowd. The Kathryn Kuhlman choir sang beautifully, and the testimonies all told of the glory of a personal encounter with God in the person of Jesus the Son. If I hadn't already known that I was immune to such things, I might have felt some of the anticipation.

I'd never heard Dave Wilkerson preach before. When he'd talked to us back at Clinton Avenue, it was always informally, sort of "person to person." I'd never heard him make like a real preacher before. I remember thinking, "He's sure got a big voice for such a little guy!"

Then suddenly I was locked in on what he was saying. What was the word he had used that had triggered my sudden response? "Phony?" Yeah! That was it! He was talking about being a phony before God. Well, I knew all about phonies; my life had been jammed full of them! But *that* didn't seem quite right to me. It wasn't *those* phonies he was talking about. He was talking about *me*.

"I'm the biggest phony of them all!" Sticking around Teen Challenge acting like I didn't want what they had. *Sure* I wanted it! Who in my shoes wouldn't want a new life? I wasn't kidding God any with my snickers and sneers. *He* knew that they just covered up for my longing to be able to cry over my sins with the others. He knew how much I longed to feel *something*.

That's when I prayed my first sincere and honest prayer. The invitation was being given by Dave; the choir was singing "He Touched Me" with a special warmth and glow. I bowed my head as respectfully as anyone there and said, "OK, Jesus, I want to ask You for something. I want what these people say You can give me. I want to be normal; I want to *feel* something again. If You are who they say You are, *show* me! Please, Jesus, *please make me cry!*

There, sitting in the crowd as the music swelled around me and countless numbers of young people were publicly declaring for Jesus by going forward, I privately witnessed the touching of my life by a strange warmth and power. My entire life began to pass before my eyes like a videotape replay. There were all the misery and poverty, all the disappointments, all the hurts. Then followed all my responses: my anger, hatred, and violence. Nothing had escaped the accurate eye of the One who had taken these pictures.

Then I became aware of a feeling of love. That warm Presence I had noticed was a gentle, loving one. I began for the first time to feel sorrow for all the things I'd done. Oh my poor Nina! And Dondi! The drugs and stealing really stung me, but nothing bit so deep into my conscience as the shame of prostitution. And still the warm glow of love persisted. As each incident was coming to my awareness, I was conscious that a tremendous miracle was taking place. Warm, salty tears were running down my cheeks. I couldn't believe it! Cookie Rivera was crying!

PART TWO

Chapter 16

ONLY THE BEGINNING

The chartered bus rattled and chugged its way along the Pennsylvania Turnpike as we returned to New York that night. In spite of brisk March winds whistling outside, the interior of the bus was warm with song and happy chatter as everyone discussed the events of the day. For those who had known me before that day, my reaction at the rally was a major topic of conversation. No one needed to tell my counselors that only the touch of the Lord Himself could have produced such a response in me. Because they knew how unfeeling, how cold and heartless I'd been, it was impossible for them to miss the significance of those tears. Many a "Praise the Lord!" was heard that night as my counselors considered this remarkable event.

My own thoughts were jumbled and confused. I knew I'd caught a glimpse of glory back there in that auditorium. Had I met Jesus? Was the warmth I'd felt His love? Was it really possible to meet Someone you couldn't see? I was still stirred up and excited from the whole experience. I compared the great sensations I was feeling to a good high, which was all I'd ever known of pleasure.

Nevertheless the whole day was already seeming quite unreal. The further the bus took me from Pittsburgh and the closer I got to New York, the more hazy were the details of that encounter. It didn't make a bit of sense—all that fuss over a few tears. Was I going crazy or something? Nothing had really changed—or had it?

By the time I had been back at Rhinebeck for a few days the whole experience seemed like a very distant, though extremely pleasant, dream. I had been led to expect that I would be a changed person after meeting the Son of God; but the change was hard to find. The only significant difference in me was one of motivation. After finding Jesus so loving, so accepting, I *wanted* to live my life His way. But I found I was still acting like the same old Cookie—angry much of the time, striking out at those around me, and as pessimistic and frustrated as ever. Where were the joy and victory that were supposed to be part of a life yielded to Jesus? Why couldn't I recapture the intense feelings I had experienced in Pittsburgh?

I thought I might be able to feel that same warmth in the chapel services; but if Jesus was there, I couldn't find Him. So I turned to the Bible in an attempt to learn more about Him, only to discover that my mind had been drugged too long. I couldn't make any sense out of the written Word. It took me three weeks just to memorize the simple message of John 3:16: "For God so loved the world . . ." Finally I tried to pray. I really *wanted* to talk with Jesus but couldn't find the words to ask Him the questions on my mind and tell Him how I felt. My mind wandered within a few minutes of trying to get in touch with Him. I found I had no inner resources, no habits of self-discipline. Concentrating on something—or Someone—apart from myself was impossible.

Discipline was a big part of the rehabilitation program. My days at Rhinebeck were planned for me from dawn to dusk to provide the order and discipline my life needed while I grew in faith. Chapel followed breakfast first thing in the morning and Bible study followed chapel. After lunch we had work details, followed by a time for private prayer and meditation—and then more work until dinner. The system that was designed to produce order and harmony seemed only to create rebellion and discord in me.

I really didn't *like* to work. Only occasionally in my early years had I tried to hold a job, and then at least I was being paid. Housework seemed especially dull and unrewarding. So who was always given those endless spiral stairs to clean? Of course I never applied the elbow grease that was expected. The minute I finished flicking the cleaning cloth over them in my usual half-hearted manner, my counselor would appear to tell me to do them over.

The counselor's name was Sharon Webb, and I didn't like her at all. She was a registered nurse who had been studying for a college degree until she happened to hear Dave Wilkerson talk about Teen Challenge at a church meeting. On the strength of his enthusiasm, she had come to New York to work as a volunteer for one summer, and had ended up joining the staff. A lifelong Christian, she was strong and secure in her faith—a good model for me to copy. Instead I felt threatened by her.

She was very pretty—tall and slender with a beautiful complexion and eyes that glowed with an inner light. I was jealous of her fresh good looks. But what made me dislike her most was her perfectionism and rigid discipline. Compared to her, I was sloppy, disorganized, and wavering in my beliefs. I resented her direction and refused her guidance. Instead of cooperating with her, I spent my time and energies making life miserable for her.

But the biggest stumbling block in my initial efforts to lead a Christian life turned out to be that same silly old rule forbidding the smoking of cigarettes. I couldn't understand why so much fuss was made over a little thing like cigarettes, when the big evil of drug addiction was already conquered. Why make life any harder than necessary? Jesus hadn't told me it was wrong to smoke, and I had a hunch there wasn't anything in the Bible about it either.

Nevertheless during rehabilitation rules were rules. I could accept them as they were and obey them, or I could reject them and leave the program. The rules were there to provide discipline, and to those in charge of administering the program there could be no middle ground. Since compromise seemed much more sensible to me, I pretended to accept the injunction against smoking but puffed away secretly by the window of my attic room whenever I could go there alone. I seldom had much opportunity to be alone until bedtime, and sending smoke signals out into the darkened skies became my nightly ritual.

The only problem with this arrangement was that ever since Pittsburgh I'd been aware of a growing conscience. Now when I began to sneak cigarettes, my conscience began to hurt; I couldn't understand why. It didn't occur to me at first that cigarettes were not the real issue. The real issues were obedience, honesty, and discipline. Were those cigarettes more important than trying to live honestly and openly? As I struggled to understand my discomfort, I couldn't shake the feeling that I was disappointing Jesus.

Eventually the pain of a burdened conscience got to be too much for me. I decided to give up smoking. First I promised myself that I'd never smoke another cigarette. That didn't work. Then I promised Jesus. I

quickly discovered it didn't matter *who* I promised; I
was powerless to keep my pledge. I hoped my failure
proved that Jesus really didn't care about it. Wasn't
He supposed to give me the power to do His will? I
tried to give myself every excuse I could, but the impression remained that Jesus wanted something from
me that I was unable to give Him.

During this struggle I felt that fate was out to get
me. For instance, on one occasion I had made it
through two whole nights without lighting up a cigarette—a new record. I was beginning to feel victori-
ous. Despite the fact that I *was* all out of cigarettes at
that time, I was feeling pretty good about my willpower. Then I went to another girl's room to help her
make her bed. When I pulled the covers up, a pack
of Marlboros fell out from under her mattress. The
cigarette shortage was over! "What the heck! Why
am I torturing myself like this?" Faced with temptation, my wonderful willpower fled. She shared her
cache with me, and I was back to clandestine cigarettes again. It looked as if I would just have to learn
to live with a smarting conscience.

At that point as I thought back over my experience
at Pittsburgh, I certainly had a lot of questions. What
good had it done me to meet Jesus? If He loved me
why didn't He help me with these problems? Apparently the only thing that had been changed in my life
the day I met Him was my mind. I *wanted* to live
better, but my behavior had not improved significantly. Was He just trying to show me how helpless I
was? That seemed cruel. He had restored my ability
to care—about Him, about myself, about Dondi. But
caring seemed to produce only more pain and frustration. Dondi was still back in the Bronx ghetto with
Nina, and I was still a rebellious, undisciplined ex-ad-

dict. What was the good of knowing Jesus if you couldn't live the life He wanted for you?

Clearly, I did not know my Lord well. While I was fussing and fuming with rules and counselors and trying to find some way to live victoriously for Him, He was drawing upon His limitless resources and power to deal with these problems in His own way.

Chapter 17

JUST SHORT OF VICTORY

I opened my eyes with a start. Had I been sleeping? I remembered lying down on the bed to think. I must have drifted off. Had I been dreaming when I heard that voice? But then I heard it again—those quiet, gentle tones that had roused me minutes before. "Cookie, I want you to work with young people." I'd never heard that voice before, but I knew instantly Who had spoken. I couldn't get over how clear the message was, how audible the sound of His voice. That Jesus should choose to talk to me was incredible, but I knew that it was really happening.

How well He had engineered the opportunity to talk to me! Normally during any free time, I would be messing around with some of the other girls, getting them into trouble along with me. But today, for some reason, I'd come to my room alone. I never took naps. But there I was, resting quietly on my bed, when the Lord spoke to me.

In awe of the warm Presence that was filling the room, I slipped to my knees beside my bed to pray. "Oh, Jesus, I'm so glad You've come again! I'm all confused and I need You. I want to do what You want, but I can't seem to live even one day at a time for You. How can I possibly help young people when I can't even handle my own life?" It was so good to be in touch with Him again that I found myself talking on and on, unmindful of time passing.

Suddenly I felt my heart grow heavy and the tears began to flow again. I was thinking of all the kids Jesus wanted to reach, and I was crying for them. I was too ignorant of spiritual matters to realize that He was giving me a burden for young people—a burden that was to provide the motivation for my life. At that time, however, I only knew that I was being made very sure that Jesus was calling me to serve Him by helping young people somewhere.

I discovered that I couldn't share that moment with anyone. I felt that no one would believe me. So I hugged the memory of it close and tried to imagine how He would work this out. Where would He send me to work with young people? To Teen Challenge? Not likely, since I was still far from a prize student in the rehabilitation program! What would I tell kids anyway? Well—I *had* been cured of heroin addiction. I could tell them *that!* Of course, I'd have to omit the little problem with cigarettes. What about Dondi? Did His plans for me include my little boy? I had a lot more questions to ask Him, but it seemed that I couldn't stay in His presence. Where did He go when He left me? And why did He have to leave?

Then He began to show me His presence in another way. I had not realized that He could be found in other people, but He began to make His presence known through those who surrounded me. Sharon was the first.

"It would take a miracle for us to get along!" I fumed. She'd been on my back all morning, with first one complaint and then another about my behavior.

"Cookie, you've been smoking in your room again. You know we can't let you get away with that."

"Oh, come off it, Sharon! I haven't had a cigarette

110

in weeks. You have a big imagination." I knew better than to lie! Why couldn't I stop myself?

"No, Cookie, I'm not imagining things. From the smell of cigarette smoke in your room right now, I'd say you just had every girl in the place in for a cigarette. Why must you drag them down to your level?"

"I'm not dragging anybody down. I told you I haven't been smoking at all. What kind of Christian are you? Always suspecting me of things. Always sneaking around checking up on me."

"Cookie, Cookie! What am I going to do with you? You only make it worse with your lies. I can't seem to get it across to you how serious your disobedience is. Don't you know that we've considered asking you to leave? Why won't you listen to us? We do want to help you, you know."

True to form, I managed to get the last word with, "So throw me out—I don't care! It isn't very pleasant living with people who don't trust you anyway." And I stomped off to my room again. I knew I was in the wrong, but I just couldn't seem to keep from arguing. I reasoned that Sharon obviously hated me and wanted to see me fail in the program. I wondered if there were any way to get rid of her.

While I was fuming and wishing her bad fortune, Sharon was asking Jesus to remove the barriers that separated us. I knew Jesus only as the warm, loving Lord of those fantastic moments of closeness with Him. I had not yet learned that He is also Lord of the upsetting times, the disagreements, the unpleasant situations. Sharon knew Him better. Whereas I could only fuss and stamp my feet in frustration, she knew how to turn the whole situation over to Jesus by a simple act of faith through prayer. I was still a baby in spiritual matters; she was more mature. Of course the God she addressed was the same God that

111

I was coming to know; but the prayers she offered up in the name of Jesus got through to Him where all my tears and rantings never could. He began to minister to our difficulties with His love and wisdom.

Not all at once, but gradually, I noticed a change in Sharon's attitude toward me. She no longer avoided me to head off conflict. Instead she began to drop by my room during quiet times and talk with me about Dondi and my concern for him, about my future, about Jesus. She stopped preaching at me about my failures and started sharing her own life with me. I no longer felt accused and threatened by her confidence in the Lord. I felt encouraged and hopeful, because she let me know that she too had known defeats in her life that He had turned into victories. And she began to share her prayer life with me.

One day she was sitting on the edge of my bed with chin propped in her hand just listening to me ramble on, when suddenly she interrupted with, "Cookie, there's something I've been wanting to tell you, but I've been waiting until I was more certain you'd understand. I've been talking to the Lord an awful lot lately about you and your future. He has shown me that He has a special assignment picked out for you. When Jesus calls you to do His work you should be ready. I'd like to pray with you about this."

Oh, wow! Jesus had told *Sharon* about wanting me to work for Him too. I hadn't imagined that voice and calling after all! As we prayed together about how He would accomplish His work through me, I was warmed again by His presence. But this time the warmth of His love was finding expression through Sharon—through her caring and her prayers for me. I began to know Sharon as my sister in the Lord, and my friend.

As my relationship with Sharon was being healed, I was painfully aware of other broken or wounded relationships in my life. Could Jesus repair the breach between me and my family? I'd written to Nina about a week after my experience at the rally in Pittsburgh and told her I had met Jesus and had decided to become a real Christian. I asked her to forgive me all the wrongs I'd done her, and said that I was sorry and wanted things to be made right between us.

I knew it would be a while before I got any answer—if I *ever* got one. Since Nina couldn't read, my uncle would have to read the letter to her. I was not at all sure she would want to hear what it said, once she realized it was from me. The last time I had seen her was some four months earlier, before I'd gone to Teen Challenge. My last words to her, as she was throwing me out of her home again, had been, "Maybe I won't have to put up with you much longer, Nina. Maybe I'll get lucky this year. You're getting pretty old. Maybe you'll do me a big favor and die soon." It had seemed a great exit line when I was high on junk, but it was a bad place to start to rebuild a feeling of kinship.

Eventually I did hear from Nina. She had someone send me a short note, saying she was glad I was happy; she was glad I'd gotten out of New York City; and she hoped I would *stay* out. She was the same old Nina, still telling me what to do. She never could resist a chance to deliver instructions, no matter how brief. But in the process of letting me know what she thought I should do, she also managed to convey the idea that she was not at all confident that I'd found any lasting answers to my problems. I was still not the most sensitive of persons when it came to putting myself in another's shoes, but I was beginning to understand how Nina might feel about me. I'd done a

113

lot to hurt her. I was actually surprised that she wrote and was satisfied with her note as a start.

Sharon had become very much aware of my despondency over my family situation, and my special concern for Dondi. We had prayed often for his safety, and for the two of us to be together in the future. However, I was not really prepared to receive God's answer.

One morning I was called in to talk with Brother Mitchell, who, together with his wife, was in charge of the girls' home. I was sure he was going to give me the boot for smoking; but when I walked into his office I found him talking with Sharon, who was grinning from ear to ear.

"Sit down, Cookie. We want to ask you something." Brother Mitchell was smiling too. The news couldn't be all bad, unless he was that happy to be getting rid of me! "Sharon here has been telling me you are burdened with concern for your son, Dondi. She thinks it's getting you down at a time when the Lord is trying to lift you up. Do you suppose it would help if you could bring Dondi out here with you?"

I couldn't believe my ears! Why would they even consider altering their carefully-structured program just for me, their biggest troublemaker? I couldn't decide whether I should laugh or cry, so I did both. "Oh, what can I say? Can he *really* come here? Oh, I don't believe it! That *would* make me so happy!"

Somehow the arrangements were made and Nina was talked into allowing him to visit Rhinebeck for a time. We were together at last! I was amazed to discover that he was a beautiful child. Was I really the mother of that chubby little boy with black, curly hair sticking out all over his head? He was a little pale, but he had the biggest, darkest eyes I'd ever seen. Surprisingly those eyes showed no trace of fear and

114

no reluctance to stay with me. He was a little shy at first; but in spite of the fact that I'd never really been a parent to him, my little boy accepted me immediately as his mother. I realized that only a miracle could have made him love and trust me. I'd certainly done nothing to deserve his affection.

Soon after Dondi arrived, I had a visit from Nina too. She couldn't resist the urge to see what Irmita was up to and to find out if I was taking care of Dondi properly. So she talked my uncle into a trip to Rhinebeck.

If I had expected that we would rush into each other's arms with kisses and tears and words of love and forgiveness, I was disappointed. It was a pleasant visit, but I found Nina still afraid to believe that the changes in me were permanent. She'd seen me through too many "cures" in the past. She was happy to see that I was happy and was satisfied that Dondi was getting good care. Beyond that she would only say, "Stay away from New York City!"

When had Nina's hair gone totally white? It was still pulled back in the old familiar bun, but there were few traces left of the dark color I remembered. And she was no longer so skinny! She was growing rounder as her years advanced. I had not really taken a good look at her in a long time. Only her tongue and her temperament remained unchanged by time. I found her sharp and bossy—not at all softened by the passing years. Still she *had* come to see me and I knew that, buried somewhere deep within her, there remained some love for me. I wouldn't have blamed her for refusing to have anything to do with me. Her visit at least opened the door to hope.

I really should have been happy then. The clash with Sharon had been resolved so beautifully! I had my son with me for the first extended period of time since he'd been born. And communication with Nina had been reestablished. Situations that had seemed impossible just a few weeks earlier had begun to resolve themselves. A loving Father was working in my life all right.

But something was still wrong. I did not yet have the love and joy in my life that I saw in other Christians—Sharon, Ruth Cowgill, Dave Wilkerson. I was still gloomy and pessimistic about everything. And I was still rebellious and undisciplined. I lacked the power to achieve a victory over my cigarette habit, and I still couldn't understand the Bible or pray the way I wanted to. I just couldn't get close to Jesus. I saw Him living in the lives of others, but what I really craved was His presence in my own life. Wasn't it enough that I loved Him? I knew He could give me whatever I lacked. But what *was* I seeking? I had no way to identify my need.

Chapter 18

BAPTISM OF LOVE

~~~~~~

Chapel service had ended, but I was still in my chair puzzling over what Brother Mitchell had said in his remarks to us that morning. He'd been talking about an encounter with the Third Person of the Godhead, the Holy Spirit. This encounter was the baptism in the Holy Spirit that I'd been hearing about ever since coming to Teen Challenge. Of course I knew that these folks, from Dave Wilkerson on down to my friend Sharon, were Pentecostals, so their beliefs were bound to be different from what I had learned in the Catholic church. I believed it was this baptism that made them so much more emotional in their worship than Catholics, and I wanted no part of that. I was born a Catholic and wanted to live as a Catholic. I felt sure I could never be a Pentecostal.

But that morning Brother Mitchell had been sharing something about the baptism in the Spirit that had awakened a new hunger in me. What was it he had said? He'd been telling us about how his life had lacked power until he asked Jesus to baptize him in the Spirit. He said he'd loved the Lord with all his heart before that, but couldn't seem to live right for Him. I sure knew *that* feeling! Then he'd gone on to say that when he received the baptism in the Spirit he'd received a baptism of love. The love of God in

Jesus had washed over, in and through him, and this same love was still present in his life every day.

"Oh, Jesus, I want that love to pour through my life. I need that power to live a life worthy of Your calling!" I was praying this way quietly when I suddenly recalled the other part of Brother Mitchell's testimony. I sat bolt upright in my chair and stopped praying. He had told how he'd received a new prayer language when he received the baptism in the Spirit. I knew this was the "speaking in tongues" Pentecostals believed in. I'd heard people speaking in tongues in every worship service I'd ever attended at Teen Challenge and they all sounded pretty much the same to me. This "language" was usually loud and always sounded like gibberish. I strongly suspected that every one of these nonsense words was made up by the speaker himself. If this was what the baptism in the Spirit did to you, then I didn't want it.

Suddenly I noticed that Brother Mitchell was approaching me with a questioning look in his eye. I jumped up and left the room quickly. I didn't want him to ask again to lay hands on me and pray for this baptism. It simply was not my style.

From the window of my room on the top floor of the house, I could see the countryside for miles around. Straight ahead were the glistening waters of the Hudson River. Groves of trees, rolling hills, and open fields were all that filled the landscape except for the river.

When I'd first arrived at this isolated old mansion in Rhinebeck, I thought it lonely and bleak. It had been winter then, and the chill grey countryside was too stark, too isolated for a city-dweller like me. But as the first signs of early spring touched the trees and grasses with bright spots of chartreuse and yellow, the view was becoming beautiful to me. I spent much time by that window trying to find the Lord in His creation. I knew He couldn't be very far away from all that beauty.

On a particularly lovely day in May I'd spent every free minute of the day by that window watching Spring arrive. Darkness found me there again. There was also a less ethereal reason for all this window-gazing. It gave me a chance to sneak a few puffs on some cigarettes. Ashamed and discouraged with my inability to conquer such a seemingly small habit, I discovered that I was actually smoking more despite all the good things that were happening in my life.

Today I'd been caught again and warned. This time suspension from the program had been dis-cussed. What would happen to Dondi and to me if we were sent back to New York City? I turned to glance at the tiny figure curled up on the bed next to mine. His cheeks had become rosy—the result of eating good meals and breathing fresh air. I'd hate to take him back to Nina's! In fact, I'd hate to go back there myself. This spacious room with its clean white walls, frilly curtains, and smooth, comfortable beds was home to me now. A crowded, rat-infested tenement didn't seem very appealing.

So why was I putting all this in jeopardy by stub-bornly continuing to break the rules? And it wasn't just the cigarettes. It was everything that required the least amount of self-control or discipline. I still couldn't follow directions or take orders gracefully. I struggled to obey, but not without some complaining or arguing every time.

Absent-mindedly I lit a cigarette and puffed a small jet of smoke out the open window, as I reflected on my life over the four months since Dutch had taken me to Clinton Avenue. "Oh, Jesus, where are You? I need You. I need Your power so much. But I

119

can't seem to find You any more. Things are still all messed up in my life. If You don't help me, I'm going to get thrown out of here—and then what will happen to us? I thank You for this place and for all the people You've sent to help me—for Sharon, for Ruth, for Dave. And I especially thank You for bringing Dondi here. But Jesus, I need more. I need Your strength. Please—I need You here *all* the time!"

Then I noticed that my cigarette, the last one in the pack, was nearly half gone, and I'd only taken one drag on it. I carefully tamped it out. If I was just going to daydream, I might as well save the cigarette until later. It would be a shame to waste the last one I had.

With a guilty start I realized the incongruity of what I was doing—praying to Jesus one moment and worrying about running out of cigarettes the next. "You are really hopeless, Cookie!" I sighed. "You don't deserve the breaks you've gotten, and all because of these stupid cigarettes you are going to lose all you've gained." As a wave of disgust swept over me, I tossed the last half-cigarette—that "insurance butt"—out the window into the dark night.

When I tried to resume my prayer, I found myself without words. Then I remembered Sharon's telling me about a man who came to accept the Lord just by repeating His name over and over. So I started calling, "Jesus, Jesus, Jesus," softly and repeatedly. Gradually a warm glow filled the emptiness within me and I found other words to say—words of love and praise.

"I love You, Jesus. I thank You and I praise You for Your goodness, Your faithfulness, and Your love. Thank You for calling me to Yourself. Praise You, Jesus! *¡Gloria a Cristo! ¡Bendito sea Tu Nombre!* Thank You for giving Your life and for dying for me.

Oh, Jesus, how I love You!" I was suddenly light-headed, almost drunk with a feeling of love for Jesus—the Son of God Himself. I felt so light, so free, I could have been floating in the air. I no longer compared the joy of His presence to a high on heroin. Heroin had never been *that* good!

Then I continued to tell Jesus how much I loved Him out loud, only I didn't understand the words I was saying. For at least half an hour I continued to worship my Jesus, using words I'd never learned and could not understand. All I knew was that they were the *right* words and that Jesus understood every one of them perfectly.

When I found that my legs were working again, I reluctantly withdrew from the window to go to bed. It was getting late, and even though I did not feel at all tired, I was sure I'd regret the lateness of the hour when it came time to get up in the morning. But once in bed, I couldn't sleep. I still felt like I was floating on a warm, soft cloud.

This must be the baptism in the Spirit! I must have been speaking in tongues! It was nothing like I'd imagined—not at all disgusting. Even though I felt really warmed by the love of Jesus and excited by His nearness, there was none of the hysterical emotionalism I'd been fearing. I just felt strong in my faith and sure of the goodness of the Lord. And I was so very conscious of my love for Him! I could find nothing wrong with a response like *that*. So I continued to talk to Jesus in Spanish, in English, and in tongues throughout the night. Still I was the first one up the next morning—fresh and raring to go. It had been a great night!

My early rising should have given everyone the first clue that something was different. I was not known for getting up easily. In fact, there had been many bad scenes over my sleeping late and many battles with those who tried to get me up. It wasn't until we were gathering for breakfast, however, that Mrs. Mitchell commented, "Well, will you take a look at the smile on Cookie this morning! Who turned on all the lights? Something pretty wonderful must have happened."

She was right. I was still glowing from a Power Source I didn't understand myself. "Well, I—er—I think I met the Holy Spirit last night," I stammered. "Does it really show?"

In the cold light of day the experience of the night seemed impossible. But I was still aglow after breakfast and on through chapel. Jesus was there in the worship service that morning, and I suddenly knew that He'd been there all along. I could hardly wait for the time when we were invited to give a word of testimony. I was the first to jump to my feet. I had so much to share, so much I wanted to tell all those beautiful people.

But no sooner had I gotten out my first "Praise the Lord!" than I found myself speechless. When I tried to speak, the only words I could say were those in the language I'd spoken during the night. How embarrassing! I was standing there speaking in tongues before the very group I'd privately ridiculed for their emotionalism. However, they were more loving and accepting than I had been. My efforts to share my new love of Jesus with them was welcomed with tears of joy and shouts of praise. Even that moment of humiliation turned into glory. Praise the Lord!

Of course the glow subsided eventually to a reasonable warm flame of love burning steadily within me, and I found I could testify to His presence in understandable languages too. I was surprised to find how much of this whole business of worshipping in the

Spirit was actually in my control. I found that, like Jesus Himself, the Holy Spirit is a patient, loving friend who does not want to coerce me or force me into a position that is unpleasant. He waits to be asked for His help.

However, it certainly was true that overnight, His very presence had made some significant changes in my spiritual life. I was stronger, more sure in my belief in Jesus as Savior. I no longer *hoped* that Jesus would help me; I *knew* He would. I was constantly aware of His presence and power. For the first time I *knew* I'd make it—that this was not just another resting place in my downhill trip. Salvation was for keeps.

Jesus also filled me with so much love and joy that my personality was permanently altered. I sang my way through work details and smiled and laughed more freely. I didn't mind taking orders so much, and my natural leadership abilities were directed into more constructive channels. No one could quite believe I was the same girl who had been so gloomy and pessimistic before. Well, I really *wasn't* the same person. I was Cookie Rivera *plus* the powerful overflow of the Spirit of God within me. Life for the first time was really *fun*.

And finally I discovered that I had an insatiable appetite for the Word of God. The Bible began to make sense to me as the Spirit opened up the meaning. I couldn't get enough of Bible study, prayer, and worship. "Why are they suddenly making the time for prayer and meditation so short?" I wondered.

I also began to wonder *why* all of this had happened to me. I had not actually asked to be baptized in the Spirit; I had run from it. No one had laid hands on me or instructed me personally in this experience. So why had Jesus gone ahead and given me what He knew all along I needed? Why didn't He do it when I first experienced difficulty in my Christian walk?

I couldn't answer those questions then and even today I can't be sure that I have all the answers. But I am satisfied that Jesus chose the *right* time and place for giving me His power to live. If I could identify anything as the trigger to my being baptized on that particular night it would have to be obedience. Tossing a half-burned cigarette out the window seemed more an impulse than an act of obedience, but it was all I was capable of doing. Along with calling on Jesus for help, it was enough. He met my small step with a giant move of His own. I was instantly delivered from bondage to cigarettes. That half-cigarette was my last. He freed me completely.

So I finally knew real victory in my Christian life. I was learning that the abundant life Jesus had promised His disciples was not just an empty phrase. Life was really exciting! For the first time ever, I looked confidently to the future. I knew there were wonderful surprises ahead. And the first was not long in coming.

Chapter 19

THE SIZE OF HIS LOVE

"You want *me* as a junior staff member of Teen Challenge?" In utter amazement and disbelief, I fairly shouted the question at Dave Wilkerson as we talked together in the office at Rhinebeck. He had come to spend the day looking over the girls' program and had sought me out for this private talk.

"Yes, Cookie, we'll need you for the summer at least. We are about to begin our summer evangelism program, and we sure would like to get into your old neighborhood in the Bronx this year for some street rallies. I've heard about the great things the Lord has been doing in your life. Do you think you are ready to share what He has done in you with some others who need to know Him?"

Was I ready? It was a good question, certainly deserving of more prayer and soul-searching than I gave it at that moment. I was more pleased and flattered than I should have been and quite sure that this was the Lord's answer to the question of where I would minister to young people. I said yes without blinking twice.

"It's settled then. Someone will bring you in to Clinton Avenue next week. We'll be ready to begin our summer work by then."

I fairly floated back to my room. I was going to be used by the Lord for His work in the ghetto after only five months in the rehabilitation program! *Me*—the worst trouble-maker they'd ever had until a couple of weeks ago. I knew it was most unusual for a girl so new in the Lord, especially one with my background, to be asked to join the staff. Most of the counselors, like Sharon, had lived a life with Jesus for many years. My ego grew more inflated by the minute.

When I got to my room, however, my feet returned to the ground with a thud. There was Dondi, all grins and vitality, playing with some toys in the middle of the room. Oh, *no!* I'd forgotten completely about Dondi. If I left Rhinebeck, he would have to go back to Nina's. He couldn't stay with me at Clinton Avenue. I had no idea how the Mitchells had managed to talk Nina into letting him come to stay with me in the first place, but I knew that his stay was considered only a temporary one. Long before, the State of New York had declared me unfit to raise him. Nina was his legal guardian. My chances of ever getting him back to keep were poor at best—but I sure didn't want to send him back to the ghetto so soon.

For a few hours I focused my thoughts on the problem so intently that I lost sight of the One Who could be trusted for the solution. I began to imagine all the worst possibilities for my son's future if he were taken from me then, and concluded that I simply couldn't allow him to return to Nina's. I began to consider slipping away from Rhinebeck with him.

Fortunately, I took a few minutes, in the midst of my scheming and plotting, to ask the Lord to bless these plans of mine. Having thus acknowledged, even though belatedly, that He had some interest and concern in this business, I was once more open to guidance and leading by His Spirit. And once again the Lord spoke to me very distinctly and quite explicitly: "Cookie, why won't you trust Me? Didn't I take care of Dondi all that time when you weren't fit to do it yourself? If I did so then, how much more can I be trusted to look after him now! Don't worry about your son. Trust *Me*. I will take care of him."

And that settled it. I could not see *how* and did not fully understand *why*, but I knew that the Lord would watch over Dondi's future and mine. Dondi returned to live with Nina, but I was released from worry. I was secure in the knowledge that Jesus had the power to do as He promised.

So it was back to the Brooklyn home of Teen Challenge on Clinton Avenue. From the freshness of a lush spring-turning-summer in the open countryside to the bleakness of an already-steaming cement city, it seemed I was traveling from one world to another.

I could have been depressed by the extreme contrast between these worlds, but my mind was preoccupied with another comparison. I was recalling a dirty, disheveled eighty-five pound junkie and prostitute who had first walked into the Clinton Avenue building just five months earlier. She bore little resemblance to the healthy-looking girl in the bright summer dress, with hair carefully combed and a glowing complexion, who was going back to the same address as a member of the staff. Like most junkies who kick drugs, I had gone through an initial eating jag to replace months and years of lost calories that my body suddenly craved again. I had gained nearly forty pounds and was remarkably changed at 125 pounds. I wondered if my old friends would know me. Not all the changes in my life had been inner, spiritual ones. Some were very obvious.

"Welcome home, Cookie! Oh, don't you look marvelous! It's so good to see you!" Ruth Cowgill's welcome was as warm and loving as ever. Her usual maternal embrace had additional warmth stemming from the recognition that I came now as a sister in Christ. I had been wondering who the Lord would send to replace Sharon in my life. How had I managed to forget the special love that He had given Ruth for me? It was indeed good to be "home."

There were many new faces at Teen Challenge that summer—clean-cut, fresh, glowing faces of young people who were giving a summer to work for the Lord in street evangelism. Most were from the Midwest. All were full of zeal for spreading the Good News of Jesus. And almost all regarded me with mixed emotions—grateful that the Lord had moved into my life, but wondering how complete my transformation was. My ego was restored to a more appropriate size when I realized that not everyone saw me as secure in the Lord. I was going to have to demonstrate the fruit of His Spirit and walk the narrow way carefully in order to gain full acceptance by all the staff members.

Of course He already knew the temptations and discipline that lay before me, so He sent, in addition to Ruth, another very special friend. Dagmar Rettedal was a tall, slender blonde of Norwegian extraction who had grown up in South Dakota. On vacation from a teaching job in Colorado, she was among those engaging young people who, led by the Spirit, were in New York City to bring the Gospel to the ghetto. Like Sharon and all the others, she had known Jesus since early childhood and radiated a sweet confidence in His goodness. Her personality was not at all like mine. She was calm and quiet and reliable, where I was restless and noisy and unpredictable. But we complemented each other. She helped me to continue growing in the Lord that first summer of my new life.

The work itself was faith-building. Our street meetings—"open-air rallies," we called them—were conducted by teams of workers. A team would go into a ghetto neighborhood, block off a street to traffic, and—using a public-address system—share the Lord Jesus in song and testimony with all who would listen. I was amazed to find that the city police were totally cooperative in such adventures. Police cooperation was a commodity I had never known, and it took some getting used to. If I hadn't already come to believe in miracles, I would have done so when I saw Officer Harris, the policeman I'd slashed in that famous street brawl, smilingly help us set up our equipment for a rally in my old neighborhood. It was a change too radical to have been humanly inspired.

The first rally in which I was to witness was a truly memorable one. We were going to my old stomping grounds, Fox Street between 163rd Street and Westchester Avenue. "Little Korea," as the area was known locally, was the toughest, most disreputable area in the entire Bronx ghetto. The residents there were considered the dregs of society—drug addicts, prostitutes, homosexuals, thieves. We used to note, without a trace of humor, that the most respectable persons in that neighborhood were the alcoholics. These were *my* people, the ones who had known me best before I'd gone to Teen Challenge. I had a lot I wanted to tell them.

"Everybody ready? Then let's go!" was the rallying cry of Dave Wilkerson as we finished praying for the success of the rally and scrambled into the big gray van that would take us to Little Korea. The day was hot and sultry and we tried to beat the heat by singing Gospel songs in Spanish and English as we sped across the Brooklyn Bridge into the Bronx. The music kept us refreshed until we arrived.

My feet had barely hit the sidewalk when I heard, "Hey, Cookie! Cookie Rivera, are *you* ever a sight to see! Where have you been? Man, how did you get so fat?" Two enormous black arms engulfed me and lifted me right off my feet. It was Sam, an old friend from the worst of my past. He *would* be the first to spot me! I was very much aware of all those innocent Teen Challenge workers standing there with mouths gaping, not quite sure what they should do.

"Put her down! She's not a bum any more; she's a woman of God." Dave's voice always seemed to boom out even when he spoke quietly, as he did then. Sam's arms slackened as he looked at me with eyes widening in disbelief.

"It's true, Sam. I belong to Jesus now. I'm clean of junk and I'm high on life. Stick around. I want to tell you all about it."

But Sam was backing off with a look of disgust on his face. He spun quickly around and disappeared into an alley.

"OK now, let's set up quickly. We have a lot to do here today!" Dave was trying hard to take the attention off me, and I appreciated his efforts. But still my face burned with embarassment. What a lousy way to kick off my first rally!

Later as our singing group harmonized on some fast-moving Gospel music, I wondered if it was possible for the Lord to move among the bedraggled people who were gathering, half out of curiosity and half in an effort to escape the suffocating closeness of the crowded tenements. As the sounds of the lively music rose into the air, heads began appearing at windows that had no panes. How would I have responded in the old days if I'd heard a group of clean-cut kids singing songs about Jesus right in my front yard?

Almost in answer to these thoughts some water balloons came whizzing down and exploded on the steaming cement. On the rooftop I spotted some Black Muslims gleefully lobbing the water-filled missiles down at the platform. "The rats!" I thought, my spirits sinking even lower. "We'll never get through to this crowd with all that commotion!"

But the crowd *was* listening. Dave had the loudspeaker and was delivering a beautiful, clear sermon about the woman caught in adultery. I'd never heard it put so simply before. When Dave got to the words of Jesus, I heard them spoken directly to me. "Go and sin no more." And suddenly it was *my* turn to talk, to share what His life had done for me. "Oh, Jesus—please give me the right words. I want them to know how much You love them." With a wary glance at the rooftop where the Muslims were poised with another barrage of balloons, I began to share what had happened to me.

"Hey—you up there on the roof, and all you people out here trying to get cool. You know me! It's Cookie Rivera! See? You know *me*, don't you, Mrs. Valdez? And you, Carmen? How about it, Joe? Remember me? I look a little different now, don't I? You want to know what's happened?" And—miracle of miracles—they *were* listening, intently. My transformation was so apparent, they *did* indeed want to know what had happened. Occasional water balloons whizzed past my head, but the crowd paid no heed.

"Well, you all know what I was. I was like a lot of you—a prostitute, a junkie, a liar, and a thief. I hated everyone. I didn't know the meaning of kindness or love.

"But I'm not like that any more. I've met the Son of God. Jesus is real. He is alive. He has made me over

131

into a new person—the one you see here today. I don't shoot junk any more. I'm high on life because Jesus has given me a life worth living. I don't have to lie and cheat and steal and sell myself to anyone. I belong to God now, and Jesus is the One Who saved me."

The tears that were always just below the surface started spilling over again, and my voice caught as I spoke. I was trying hard not to cry. I knew that to this group of people tears were a sign of weakness. They would think that Jesus had made me weak, not strong; and I certainly didn't want that. But try as I might, I could no longer hold back the tears. Whereas in the past I had been incapable of all emotion, now I was incapable of stifling my feelings.

The others on the platform were crying too, as were many of those silent, staring people before me. Before that moment, tears might have been a sign of weakness in this neighborhood, hardened as it was by sin, but right then tears signified spiritual strength. The Lord had given me those tears for a purpose. They unlocked doors in hearts that had long been closed to God. As the people shared my tears of thanksgiving and joy, they were tearing down barricades and opening up their own lives to His love. Later even the Black Muslims came down for prayer. I'd never seen anything like the crowd's response. I knew that the Holy Spirit was working overtime that day. No human effort alone could have had such an effect on that sin-toughened group of people.

I saw that same remarkable response many times that summer—but never again did it surprise me the way that first rally did. I had known the Lord of Lords personally in my own life. I had seen His power deliver me from drugs and bring me discipline and self-control. But I still had failed to comprehend the size of His love and His concern for all people. That first summer of my new life, the God I loved was magnified many times over in my eyes.

Chapter 20

MUCH TO LEARN

Had the entire summer consisted only of street rallies, I would have been completely satisfied. But I would not have grown. I was there to learn as well as to serve that summer. And I still had much to learn.

At first I shared some of the concern the staff felt about my newness in the Lord. I had never been subjected to real temptation with regard to drugs since my arrival at Clinton Avenue with One-Eyed Dutch. I'd been kept safe in the isolation of Rhinebeck, where all the inventiveness I possessed had been needed just to keep me supplied with cigarettes. But what would it be like back in the city, where drugs were a mere stone's throw away? Had I been truly delivered? Or would the old desires be aroused by proximity?

I had not long to wait for an opportunity to test my strength. The young volunteers who manned the program that summer were all totally ignorant of the ways of the people they were there to reach for Jesus. As a qualified expert, I became something of a guide to them in this foreign land. I took them out to the various neighborhoods to meet the people and to view firsthand the ugliness of the entire ghetto life. One day we decided it was time for them to see an actual shooting gallery.

There were about five of us—three boys and two

girls—who took the bus to the Bronx that day. I knew some places where we would find someone shooting junk almost any hour of the day. The enemy could be observed close up.

As we started down the dimly lit stairs to the tenement basement, I was hit by a sudden stab of fear. Was I going to be tempted by the sights below? Could I take it, seeing someone shoot my old friend heroin into his veins? Was I truly free of that living hell called addiction, or had I just been kidding myself?

I was surprised to find myself surveying the scene in that basement with cool detachment—almost as if I were watching a play unfolding on a distant stage. Not a prop was missing. Grey walls splattered with human filth, grey floors piled with human litter, and grey lumps of humanity lying there empty of human dignity and almost oblivious to our presence. Even the rats were grey.

And the smells! Body odors of the worst kind mingled with the burt-straw smell of marijuana smoke, the acrid scent of vomit, and the sickening smell of heroin burning in little cups. We could feel, rather than smell, the combined stench hitting us: a force stronger than mere odor. I had feared I might be tempted by the sights there; instead I was repulsed by what I saw and what I *smelled*. Why? Just five months before I would have been there desperately jabbing a needle in my own vein. Suddenly I realized I was no longer the Cookie Rivera who *had* been. I came to that old haunt with new eyes, new desires. Old things had indeed passed away, and I was a new creature.

At that time I knew beyond any doubt that Jesus had delivered me once and for all from the temptation of drugs. Heroin no longer had any power over me. I was lost for a moment in the impact of that discovery, in the great love that swept over me as I realized the immensity of the miracle the Lord had worked in me.

Then I looked around and saw Noah cooking up his fix. Several of my old sidekicks were there that day, but the Spirit seemed to lead us all to pray for Noah. We prayed that Jesus might reach out to him as He had to me, and that in His power another new life might begin.

We never knew if that prayer was answered. Once his desperate need for heroin had been met, Noah became talkative, apologetic, eager—whatever he thought we wanted him to be. He gave his works to one of the fellows in our group without thinking twice about it. I knew that a junkie who is that high is as immune to the message of Jesus as any person on the face of the earth.

Whether or not our visit to the shooting gallery bore fruit in Noah's life, the young people who were there that day at least got a glimpse at the world they could only have guessed at before—and I gained a new awareness of the freedom that was mine in Christ.

By that time, I very much needed that assurance. I was continually being reminded of the fact that I was still not totally accepted by the entire staff at Teen Challenge. I would overhear a whispered warning before we'd leave for a street meeting, "Keep an eye on Cookie"—and I would be deeply hurt by the lack of trust it revealed. I tried to reason, "Of course they worry about me. They *care* about me and don't want to lose me back to this sordid world." But still I couldn't help being shaken by their lack of confidence in me—which I felt reflected a distrust of the female addict in general. Was it possible that I was the *only* one who knew that Jesus could heal the female junkie as totally and completely as He could heal male addicts?

As if to confirm my growing conviction that I was indeed alone in this belief, I learned that the girls' home at Rhinebeck had been closed, and the girls in the rehabilitation program there had been sent home. The reason given was that the mansion was being converted into a Bible school. The *real* reason, I felt, was that the female rehabilitation program simply had not borne the expected fruit. So far I was the most encouraging product of that ministry—and obviously my associates on the staff weren't yet convinced that the change in *me* was permanent.

I might not have made it through that summer if it hadn't been for Ruth and Dagmar. Dave and Don Wilkerson gave me vital encouragement and counsel too, but at that point in my rehabilitation I needed to be accepted and trusted by other women. I needed the understanding only a woman could give me—a woman who could love me through all the pain of recovery. God saw my need and gave me, not one, but two women who could minister to it.

Ruth compensated in a way for the mother I never really had. She wanted for me all that a mother would want for her child, and she spared no effort on my behalf. I knew I could always count on the wisdom of her advice and the steadfastness of her love. Just as I considered Dave Wilkerson my spiritual father, I thought of Ruth as my spiritual mother.

But Dagmar—quiet, shy Dagmar, with her ability just to *be* there to lean on—really saw me through the worst of my crises. There came a time when I was completely at odds with some of the men on the staff. One in particular, an ex-addict himself, seemed to me to regard all female addicts as hopeless cases. I was not yet mature enough to handle what looked to me like rank prejudice in the name of the Lord, and the unavoidable confrontation between us occurred. After letting him have it with all the fury of my Puerto Rican temper, I fled the building, intending to run away and never return.

Ruth ran after me, calling my name. I was afraid she would fall, running on the rough sidewalk in her high-heeled shoes, and I went back with her just to keep her from being hurt. At the first opportunity, however, I slipped away and got on a subway. At the first stop I got off and sat in a park for five hours or more, just thinking and trying to figure out what Jesus would have done in my shoes.

An addict who knew me saw me sitting there, and stopped to talk. I couldn't resist pouring out my grievances against the Teen Challenge staff into his sympathetic ear. He tried to talk me into chucking the whole thing and going with him to get a piece of the action. It would have been so easy—instead, I called Clinton Avenue and asked for Dagmar.

"Cookie, where *are* you? Oh, praise the Lord you're all right! We've been praying all afternoon for you. Let us come get you. *Please* come on home!"

It had been a close call—too close! But, because of that moment of testing, I had some idea of the strength of the bond that held me to Jesus. I had a lot to learn yet about "loving the unlovable," but I had learned that His strength is sufficient for temptation. Going back dealt quite a blow to my pride—but even that was to prove a valuable lesson in days to come.

Chapter 21

GROWING PAINS

Before the end of the summer, I had come to the conclusion that the Lord wanted me to go to Bible school—*me*, a tenth-grade drop-out. Dagmar had joined me in prayer about this and confirmed my impression with a witness of her own. She went with me to present my case to Dave Wilkerson.

To his credit, he heard me all the way through before coming to the point in his always direct and concise way. "Cookie, I think you are rushing the Lord a little. You haven't even been through a full rehabilitation program yet. It's too soon to take on additional pressures of study and discipline. Besides, we really don't have the money to send you away to school this year. I think you should wait until the Rhinebeck school opens. We'll make a place for you there."

The matter should have ended at that point. I had too great a respect for Dave's wisdom and counsel to want to argue with him about my plans. But to my confusion the impression persisted that I should make plans to attend Bible school right away. Dagmar had the same impression, and she wanted to take me to her home in Colorado and try to raise some money for my tuition for a Spanish-American Bible school in El Paso, Texas that my old friend, Nicky Cruz, had told me about.

So we went again to see Dave. Partly to placate me

and partly because Dave has such a healthy respect for the leading of the Spirit in anyone's life—including mine—he agreed to lay out a fleece, like Gideon of the Old Testament to discover the will of God. "OK," he said. "If someone calls between now and next Tuesday, when Dagmar is ready to leave for Denver, and offers to sponsor Cookie in Bible school for one year, I will accept it as God's sign that He wants her to go to school this year. If no one calls, I can't in good conscience let her go."

"No one knows me or knows I want to go to school," I thought angrily; "so who would make such a crazy offer?" That was Wednesday. On Friday the phone rang. It was the Christian couple who had driven Dutch and me to Teen Challenge months earlier. They felt that the Lord wanted me to go to school, and they offered to sponsor me for one year. Impossible as it had seemed to me, the Lord had made His will known. Dave accepted the couple's offer as God's answer to his fleece and sent me off with his blessing.

When Dagmar and I left New York City in August, I had exactly ten dollars to my name and a cardboard box with two changes of clothing in it. But I also had the promise of God that I was to attend school that year and a pledge of support from the couple who had already done so much for me.

Strangely enough, the money offered by those wonderful people never materialized. Financial reverses made it impossible for them to sponsor me. By the time I received that disappointing news, however, I was quite sure the Lord would provide. And of course He did.

The remainder of the summer I spent with Dagmar and her brother-in-law, who was the minister of a Full

Gospel church in Denver. Through his connections and efforts on my behalf, many churches asked us to come and share with their members our experiences in the Teen Challenge ministry. The offerings that were collected paid my tuition and travel expenses to the school in El Paso.

The Lord taught me a lot more about His love while I was in Colorado. Although I had gotten over my prejudice against Blacks during my years as a junkie, I still held on to some funny notions about Caucasians. I felt that their attitude toward Puerto Ricans was on the whole patronizing and unaccepting. That summer I learned that this generalization was inaccurate. Jesus poured such love and caring through the wonderful Midwesterners I met that summer that I was to live off their fellowship in the Spirit for many months to come. It was as if the Lord was building me up for a future trial. Within a few months I knew the wisdom of His planning.

One of the Caucasians who showed God's love to me in Colorado was a Baptist seminary student by the name of John Oldfield. He helped us get invitations to several churches, and often drove us to meetings in his car. I had not known him long when I decided he would be a perfect husband for my friend Dagmar, and I began to play Cupid. Before I left Denver, I predicted to both of them that they would be married within the year. I managed only to embarrass Dagmar with such a bold prediction, since they weren't even dating then.

The time had come for me to make my plane reservations for the flight to El Paso when I received a phone call from Dave Wilkerson. "Cookie, look—I need you in Pittsburgh by September 5. There's going to be another big youth rally, and we want them to hear your story. We'll pay your plane fare from Denver to Pittsburgh and then from there to El Paso. Just get to Pittsburgh by the fifth!"

So it was that a scant six months after my conversion at the Syria Mosque in Pittsburgh, I found myself on stage in that same building. When the choir sang "He Touched Me" just for me, the tears I shed were tears of joy instead of remorse. My Lord was so good, so powerful, so loving! I knew I was undeserving of Him.

Sharon had sent along a trunk to Denver containing several dresses for me, and Dagmar had presented me with some new shoes as a going-away present. When I boarded the plane in Pittsburgh, heading for El Paso, I felt like a woman of real substance. My cardboard box had been replaced with Sharon's trunk, and in my pocket were four hundred dollars the Lord had provided through His people in the Denver area—more than enough for tuition. The God Who had called me to go to school was not sending me off penniless.

No one rushed forward to greet me when I arrived at the airport in El Paso, although the Reverend Mr. Sanchez, the director of the school, was there waiting for me. I hadn't included a picture in my application to the school, and the mental image he carried of me bore no resemblance to the actual Cookie. When we finally met and identified each other, his expression was one of astonishment. "Well, Cookie Rivera, I have some young ladies who are just dying to meet you!" Then he chuckled and added, "I don't believe it! *You're* Cookie Rivera!"

His greeting had been warm enough, but I was somewhat baffled and unnerved by his obvious amusement. *What* didn't he believe? And *who* wanted to meet me? Many questions churned through my mind as we drove to the school.

142

The "young ladies" turned out to be girls who would be sharing a dormitory with me. As soon as we arrived at the school, each girl, without exception, arrived in the doorway looking pale and anxious, then burst into a giggle when I was introduced. Again I wondered what was so funny. Finally one of the girls let me in on the joke. "You should have sent a picture!" she giggled. "When we heard that Cookie Rivera was a former gang leader and a drug addict, we imagined a bigger girl, someone mean-looking. I guess we allowed our imaginations to run away with us."

Since I was back down to my normal weight of 105 pounds and stood only five feet two, I certainly was not a very formidable figure. I had to laugh too. But the realization was dawning that I came from a background that was a world apart from El Paso, Texas—a background that these girls could not hope to understand. Right then I began to feel the first pangs of homesickness for New York—for Ruth and Sharon and Dagmar. Why had Jesus led me to this place where I'd be among strangers? Was I going to be alienated once again, as I had been in my early years?

Certainly the girls at the school were quite different from what I'd imagined. For one thing, they were all so young—eighteen or nineteen, and fresh out of high school. Many of the girls were daughters of ministers, and all had been raised in strict Christian homes. Without exception, my classmates were sweet, untarnished virgins who were ignorant of any way but their own. By contrast I was twenty-three, an unwed mother, and anything but innocent. I felt instantly out of place. I could not envision close Christian friendships growing out of contact with such naive youngsters.

I also discovered shortly after my arrival that not

143

everyone who attended Bible school was necessarily motivated by a desire to serve the Lord. Many of the girls seemed to be putting in time while waiting to marry a nice Christian boy. I suspect that many of them thought I was a bit strange, with my ideas of serving God. I began to suffer the old familiar pangs of feeling different from all who surrounded me.

The school environment didn't help to make me feel at home. Somehow I had imagined that the Bible school would have grand imposing buildings on grounds that would be at least as spacious and well groomed as those I remembered at Rockland State Hospital in New York. Instead I found an impoverished institution, isolated from the city itself. The squat, one-storied buildings were the exact color of the dusty, tan desert surrounding them. I had become accustomed to the tall, crowded-together buildings of New York City. To me, the school seemed flat and ugly.

Before I had become accustomed to feeling once again out of place in my environment, another unhappy part of my history was repeated. I found myself the victim of another language barrier.

Early in the term I was asked to speak in chapel, to the entire student body. The school had never before had a female student with my background, and the administrators wanted me to tell my story to the students. It looked like a very easy assignment. I had spent the entire summer sharing my life story with other people, and in New York City I had done such testifying under the poorest of conditions before the most sin-hardened individuals. It always frightened me to face a large group of strangers, but my certainty that these students already knew the Lord made me feel at ease. Sharing Him with such a body of believing Christians seemed simple enough.

144

Before the assembled group, I prayed that God would use me for His glory; then I told my story with all the enthusiasm and zeal I possessed. I don't know whether anyone was touched by Jesus through that testimony. I only know that I became increasingly aware of suppressed laughter and furtive side-glances as I spoke. The only person who said anything to me about my talk after chapel was the grammar teacher. Her comment was, "I think you need to join my class."

What had I done? What had caused the students' amusement and the teacher's cryptic remark? My questions found answers as I became the brunt of much teasing and ridicule for my manner of speaking. The Spanish taught and spoken in this Spanish-American school was grammatically correct: the pronunciation, perfect. I had learned to speak correct Spanish in the Catholic school back in Caguas, but had traveled quite a distance since my school days in Puerto Rico. I didn't realize how much of the broken English and hybrid Spanish of the New York ghetto had been absorbed into my speech. During the summer, when I had testified to the people of Little Korea, my language had been readily understood. There I spoke the language of the people. In Bible school the same way of speaking was a foreign language.

I had amused the students and horrified the faculty members that day in chapel by using words that were neither Spanish nor English. The correct word for "roof," for example, is *techo*, but I had referred to *roofos* in my talk. "Weekends," which should have been *fin de semanas*, became *los weekenes*. We had invented words like that to fill in gaps in our strange ghetto slang and they had become part of my regular vocabulary.

Thereafter, of course, I made an effort to speak

only correct Spanish. But it was too late to avoid the gibes of the students who had heard me. Burdened as I was by my past and by the contrast between it and that of my fellow students, I was too sensitive to such joking. It upset me much more than it was intended to.

Occasionally I wavered in my conviction that the Lord had actually placed me there in that Bible school. Instead of the close friendships I desired, I was encountering separation from others. Instead of being free to live the new life Jesus had given me, I seemed bound to my past. The rules of the school were endless; the discipline more exacting than I had ever known. More than once I was tempted to leave—to go back to New York, where at least *some* folks understood me.

The curriculum requirements alone were an almost irresistible temptation to quit. I discovered that I was going to be studying doctrinal theology, grammar, homiletics, biblical geography, Old Testament I, and typology from the Old to the New Testament.

Whatever did the Lord have in mind? Had he brought me to school to fail in order to teach me humility? Doctrinal theology would certainly do the trick! I had never finished high school, and for eight years I had been messing up my brain with all kinds of drugs. Such heavy subjects weren't possible for someone like me.

Clearly I was going to need miraculous help from the Lord. Out of this realization and the desperation of my desire to succeed for Him came the discipline that enabled me to survive the year.

In addition to increasing my prayer time, I began to fast one day a week. Somewhere I had heard that fasting adds some kind of special power to prayer. I knew that some of the counselors back at Teen Challenge had fasted whenever a particularly great need arose or when a junkie with extraordinary problems wanted help. I myself had been the object of many fastings before I had accepted Jesus. I did not really understand the reasoning behind such a discipline, but at that point I was willing to try anything.

Wednesday was the day I set aside for fasting. From dawn each Wednesday until the same time on Thursday, I abstained from food and prayed the entire time I was not in class. At first I felt a little foolish. What possible good did it do me to go hungry one day a week? Why would the Lord honor such an effort? But slowly I began to feel a new closeness with Jesus and a gradual increase in mental ability. I still had to work long and hard at my studies, but I knew that my mind was being healed. The Spirit unlocked spiritual truths and made it possible for me to retain what I learned. The more I fasted, the more I praised Jesus for His healing touch on my brain. I knew that a miracle was taking place.

Too late did I discover that Wednesday was the only day of the week when the main course at dinner in the dining room was something other than chili. Since I had already made a vow to Jesus to fast on Wednesdays, the only meat I tasted during my entire year in that school was the few morsels found in chili. Compared to the blessings I received through this discipline, however, the sacrifice seemed very small.

By the time Christmas approached, life at the school had become at least tolerable. I was far from happy, but I realized that I was learning a great deal and was growing up spiritually. Still I was homesick: I missed Dondi; I missed New York; I missed all my wonderful close friends. Dagmar and Sharon had been faithful in writing and Dagmar called fre-

147

quently too—but their letters and phone calls could never replace the wonderful closeness we had shared praying together. I was hungry for fellowship.

The school always shut down entirely for the Christmas holidays, but by two weeks before vacation I still had no place to go. My funds were so low that a trip to New York and back was out of the question. I was feeling very much alone and forgotten when I received Dagmar's letter containing my bus fare to Denver, and an invitation to spend the holidays with her family. Jesus had not forgotten me or my need for love and fellowship. His Christmas present to me was the first real Christmas of my life.

Chapter 22

STRONGER FOR MY TRIALS

Never had Dagmar looked more beautiful to me than she did at the moment I stepped off the bus in Denver. We hugged each other and shouted, "Praise the Lord!" as tears of joy ran down our cheeks. Had it been only four months since I'd said a tearful good-bye to my friend? It seemed much longer! But how short was the trip from Denver to Sioux Falls, South Dakota, in Dagmar's car! Even though we chattered like magpies all the way, we still hadn't run out of conversation when we arrived at her parents' home.

I had never met Dagmar's family, except her brother-in-law in Denver; but that Christmas they became my second family. On Christmas Day the entire Rettedal clan came together for a family feast. I had never seen such an abundance of love expressed so freely. As love passed from one member of the family to another, I found myself soaking up the warmth.

When the time came for opening Christmas presents, I found that each and every member of the clan—even the tiniest child—had a gift for me. Afterwards, we gathered around a magnificent Christmas tree to celebrate the birth of our Savior with carols of joy. I felt completely surrounded by love and a sense of belonging. As I listened to Dagmar's sweet, lyrical soprano blending with the deep bass of her brothers' voices and the piping tones of the children, I discovered I'd never been happier in my life.

Then I began to wonder where I had been at that time the year before. Out on the streets hustling for a fix? That seemed a pretty good guess. Probably I had not even known what day it was; they had all seemed alike then, ugly and monotonous. My mind drifted further yet into the past and recalled a teen-aged girl singing Christmas carols while strapped to a bed of ice. But she had not then known the Savior of whom the songs spoke, and the carols had no more meaning for her than the words to "Jingle Bells." The sudden recognition of how wretched my life had been and how far the Lord had brought me was too much for me. I ran to a bedroom, where I could be alone to cry out my love to Jesus. My "family" understood my emotions and allowed me the privacy to express them. As a background to my tearful prayers I could hear their voices caroling, "Joy to the world, the Lord is come!" Surely no other person on earth that day knew as well as I the joy that Jesus brought to the world in His coming.

When I returned to school, I found that I would be needing every bit of the love and strength that God had provided for me during the holidays. My feelings about the school were the same, only more so. I still felt different from the other students; I still could not find understanding friends in the Lord; and I still found the strict rules and discipline hard to take. Jesus was trying to show me that He was my strength in all things, but I was very slow to learn the lesson.

Almost immediately, I found myself embroiled in some disagreeable business with a few faculty members. Many of the churches and service groups in the communities surrounding El Paso had heard about my conversion at Teen Challenge, and they wanted to hear my story first hand. As requests came in to the school for me to talk with one group or another, I looked around for some singing talent to round out my presentation. Three girls who sang in the school choir were willing to work on some arrangements. Although I had no real vocal talent myself, I do have an ear for a good sound—and they had it!

It wasn't long before I ran into opposition from some of the faculty members, who seemed to resent the popularity we were acquiring outside the school. More and more frequently, special activities were scheduled on nights when we had a meeting. Like the elder brother in the parable of the prodigal son, these lifelong Christians could not understand why God should give such recognition to someone like me, who had done such awful things in the past. They had lived a lifetime playing it straight, but no one asked *them* to talk to groups about their lives. Later in my spiritual growth I became more understanding of such a viewpoint. But I was still new in my faith. They just made me furious!

One day I could take it no longer. A special activity was called as we were practically ready to walk out the door for a meeting. My patience snapped, and I exploded. As my fury burned within, I went to my room and packed my trunk. I had decided I could not submit to such treatment a minute longer.

I got as far as El Paso, where I spent the weekend praying at a friend's house. As I asked Jesus to show me His answers to these problems at the school, I began to realize that I had behaved like a spoiled child, stomping off in anger as soon as the situation got tough. The Lord held a mirror before me that long weekend, and the reflection was humiliating.

But in spite of this fresh insight, I still found it extremely difficult to go back to the school and apologize for my behavior.

As I got on the bus and headed back towards school, I recalled the day when I had to swallow my pride and go back to Teen Challenge after a similar fracas. Why did it seem even harder this time? Was it because I could think of no friend I'd be returning to who could help ease the pain of defeat? In my mind I was sure that those teachers were in the wrong; but in my heart I knew that Jesus wanted me to forgive them and seek forgiveness for myself. He finally had His way.

Imagine my surprise when the Reverend Mr. Sanchez welcomed me back with warmth and affection. Instead of the scorn and rejection which I had expected, I received encouragement from faculty members who had never seemed to notice me before. I discovered that some of the teachers really cared about me and understood my difficulties better than I had thought. I became an instant believer in the promise that God works all things for good to those who love Him. He had taken one of my biggest mistakes—running away from school—and used it to show me His love in the very people I was running from.

From that point on, my attitude toward the school began to change. I found it easier to put up with some of the negative attitudes I encountered, and with the school discipline. I felt led to give a tenth of the offerings I received at the various churches where I spoke to the people who criticized me most. On one occasion when we received an unusually large offering—almost two hundred dollars—we gave the entire sum to the Reverend Mr. Sanchez to buy a new door for the dining hall. Gradually the pressures on me subsided, and acceptance replaced criticism and misunderstanding. The witnessing that I was led into for the Lord continued without further hindrance.

Even the regimented existence, with a precise hour set aside for this and a carefully measured moment for that, grew gradually more tolerable. Until the day I left school I could always be counted on to discover some unknown rule after I had already broken it, but my demerits accumulated more slowly as the term advanced. The Lord even gave me a measure of victory over my temper. I'd survived the testing and the heat of refining, and discovered I was stronger for my trials.

When the second term came to an end in May, I discovered that I had finished the year with the highest grades of any girl in the school and the second highest in the entire student body. When Jesus healed my mind, He did His usual first-rate job!

Nevertheless, I was not really reluctant to bid farewell to the school at the end of that term. I would eventually look back on my experiences at Bible school and see the Lord's purpose in sending me there. I had survived the test, but the refining process had been painful, and I was looking forward to going home.

Because I still didn't have the funds for transportation to New York, I accepted a series of speaking engagements along the way and trusted Jesus to supply the means to keep me traveling. Churches in El Paso, Houston, and Dallas responded generously to my story of the love that God has for junkies and prostitutes. I told the same story in Shreveport, Knoxville, and Chattanooga. By the end of my stay in Chattanooga, I finally had money enough for my plane fare to New York, with a slight detour through Denver.

Midway through the second school term, an excited, breathless Dagmar had called to tell me that my matchmaking had borne fruit and my prediction had proved accurate: she and John Oldfield were engaged and would be married in June. Although Dagmar was anything but calm, cool and collected when she phoned, she had not been too befuddled to ask me to be a bridesmaid in her wedding. I considered it a high privilege to be at her side as my dear friend married the man God had chosen for her.

After the wedding I flew directly to New York City, where a position in the summer evangelism program was waiting for me at Teen Challenge.

I was twenty-four years old and had known Jesus personally for one year and three months. What a relief to have Him in charge! I was delighted to find that He was leading me home.

Chapter 23

DEMI

━━━━━━━━━━━━━━━━━━━━━━━━━━━━━━━━

When had the Brooklyn center of Teen Challenge become home to me? I couldn't answer that question; but when I arrived back in New York City, I knew I was headed for Clinton Avenue. A phone call brought a staff member out to the airport to meet me. I never even thought about going to Nina's. Her apartment was Dondi's home until I could provide a better one for him, but it would never again be home to me.

The staff of the center welcomed me back warmly. Old friends from the previous summer were on hand, and some new staff members had been added. One was the Reverend John Benton, who was operating another Teen Challenge program for female addicts. A building across the street from the center had been set aside for this ministry, and he and his family lived there.

I was asked to live in the girls' home and to be a kind of counselor to those who were going through the program that summer. I was not quite as poised and self-assured as I felt a counselor should be, and I had had no formal training for this kind of work, but I accepted the challenge eagerly. Having so recently come through the rehabilitation program myself, I was full of ideas and insights that I felt could help others in the same situation. The summer stretched out before me full of promise and excitement. It really was good to be home!

As an added and somewhat unexpected bonus, Dondi was with me once again! Since the Bentons had a boy about his age, the staff decided that Dondi should be allowed to share my quarters for the summer. At first Nina was very reluctant to agree to this plan. She still wasn't convinced that I had changed so completely as to be 100 percent trustworthy, even after a year away at school. But she was still on welfare and was having a struggle to make ends meet. With Dondi away for the summer, she'd have fewer expenses and better opportunities to get work. Eventually economic considerations overcame caution, and Nina gave her consent for my son to live with me in Brooklyn.

Dondi turned six that summer and would start school in the fall. He was nothing like the baby I remembered having with me at Rhinebeck. When had he gotten so tall? It seemed to me he'd grown more than a year's worth since I had seen him last summer. Seeing him so grown-up looking made me think: "I've missed half of his childhood already. Lord Jesus, how much longer will it be before I can really be a mother to this child?"

While in El Paso, I had received a notice from the State of New York that I had been declared fit to be a mother and could ask for custody of my child. However being *fit* to care for my child and being *able* to do so were not quite the same thing. My future plans were too unsettled to claim him then. How would I support him? Could I expect Teen Challenge to make a permanent home for both of us? And what kind of life would he have with a mother who was a reformed junkie and whose only talent seemed to be telling others about her Reformer?

No—I needed more time to get my own life in order before I assumed full responsibility for Dondi's life. I found myself praying constantly for us to be together in the future. Much later, the memory of my own despair at having to leave my child in the ghetto while I was getting my life together would play a part in shaping the work that Jesus was calling me to do. But I didn't realize back then how well He was laying the groundwork for future years of service.

As I settled into the work at Teen Challenge that summer, I felt that I'd never really been away. However, there were many new faces among the staff members at the center. In addition to more of those great youngsters from the Midwest, with their tireless energy and evangelical zeal, there were other former addicts who were "junior staffers" like me. Among them was a fellow named Demi Rodriguez. I caught myself giving him a more-than-casual appraisal. His dark good looks did rate a second glance, but his attitude was what impressed me most. He didn't seem as condescending to the girls in the program, or to me, as most of the other fellows who had been addicts themselves. So many of these guys seem to regard me with an attitude of superiority that I had about decided no male ex-addict, even a Christian, would ever accept a female ex-addict as being on an equal basis with him. Apparently a woman's past *did* make a difference to these men, who knew it all too well. It seemed that the double standard operated even among converts.

But Demi was different. He seemed to treat me with the same respect and consideration that he displayed toward the well-brought-up young ladies who were working in the summer program. I wondered if it was his maturity that made him different. (He was

157

thirty-five.) He too had spent the previous year in a Bible school, and before that he had been at the farm in Rehrersburg, Pennsylvania, where he was rehabilitated after fourteen years of addiction to heroin. I wanted to get to know him better, but there seemed to be little chance for that. The rule was that counselors could not date each other. Anyway, I wasn't looking for any kind of attachment to a man. I felt that my years on the streets had killed any possibility of a normal marriage for me.

That summer, I was too busy to have time to fight against the rules. Within two weeks of my return, we were back in the worst of neighborhoods sharing the love of Jesus with all who would listen. And when I wasn't at a rally, I was busy counseling my girls—the ones who were going through the program that summer. And in order to continue to grow spiritually, I myself had to have time for worship and study alone. The days were too short for all that filled them.

Dondi seemed very happy to be with me: He was thriving on all the adult attention he was receiving from the workers at the Center, and he and young Jimmy Benton had struck up quite a friendship. One afternoon, while I was in chapel with the other staff members, he was outside playing with Jimmy. I was too deep in prayer to hear my name being called. Then I felt a hand on my shoulder and heard someone saying, "Cookie, you'd better come outside. There's been an accident!"

As I ran out the door, I heard Dondi screaming, "Mommy! Mommy! Help me, Mommy!" And then I saw him, lying crumpled and bleeding in the street, where a passing car had tossed him.

I began to pray as I ran to his side, "Jesus, help him! Don't let my little boy die!" Then Dave and

Don Wilkerson were beside me, and we all laid hands on him and prayed.

At once I knew he was going to be OK. I recalled the promise that Jesus had made to me that He would take care of my son for me. In light of His promise, it was unthinkable that Dondi would not recover from his injuries. Even during the frantic ambulance ride to the hospital, when he stopped breathing and required resuscitation, I never doubted that Jesus would take care of him. The real miracle was the faith and calmness the Lord gave me through a time when I otherwise might have panicked.

Dondi had a compound fracture of one leg which required an immediate trip to the operating room; but the doctors later assured me that he would be all right. His other injuries were mostly cuts and bruises that would require only time to heal.

Once my concern for Dondi was relieved, I began to worry about Nina. I'd had Dondi with me for only two weeks. I knew Nina would see this accident as evidence that I couldn't take care of him properly. Maybe she was right! Maybe he didn't belong in Brooklyn at Teen Challenge. The more I thought about it, the more depressed I became.

Strangely enough it was Demi Rodriguez who headed off the impending storm with Nina. The day of the accident, he took the van and rounded up my entire family, as many as he could find—Nina, my aunt and uncle, even my mother, whom I hadn't talked to in years—and brought them to Clinton Avenue. There in the chapel he led all of them in prayer for Dondi's recovery. Demi didn't realize the size of that miracle, because he didn't know that few of my family members were even on speaking terms with each other, let alone with God! It was another case of the Lord's working all things for good. When I heard what had happened, I couldn't believe it!

The next day, when I knew Dondi was out of danger, I agreed to leave his bedside and return to Teen Challenge. Demi and some of the "Collegians"—the Gospel singers on the summer team—were in the van that came to pick me up, but before I knew what was happening, Demi and I were alone. He had been instructed by the Collegians to take me out to Chinatown for dinner. It seemed that others liked to play Cupid as much as I did.

I guess that could have been called our first date, if dating had not been against the rules. In spite of my concern for Dondi, it was a wonderfully relaxing evening. Demi was great fun to be with. He laughed at the same things that amused me; yet he could be serious too. I enjoyed being treated so politely. Clearly he did not find good manners demeaning, as did so many men I had known. But best of all, he was able to share with me his deep, abiding faith in the same Lord I worshipped. I felt happy in his company in the same way I had felt happy in the Rettedal home at Christmas. The tensions of the preceding days had vanished.

After that we found many excuses to bump into each other in the course of a day. Since Demi drove the van on Sundays when we took the Spanish-speaking girls to church, I also got to see him then. The girls noticed that our attention was not always on them, and they teased us unmercifully. Nevertheless, before other members of the staff we tried to observe strict decorum. Although I felt a little guilty about enjoying his company—rules were still rules—I found myself constantly looking for ways to be around him. Demi was not backward about furnishing such opportunities.

I didn't allow myself to think what this mutual attraction might lead to, since I had no plans for marriage. Until I met Demi, I'd been sure that I could never feel anything for a man—that Jesus alone would be the object of my love. I had reasoned that no man would want me anyway, in view of my past. All this prior reasoning, however, did not keep me from being very much attracted to Demi. I wondered what on earth I was thinking of, acting like a teen-ager with a crush. Didn't I realize that two ex-addicts made a bad combination?

"Of course," I reasoned, "Demi is not the average ex-addict. He never was down and out. He's from a good family and when he was on drugs he managed to support his habit by honest employment." Still I felt I was asking for trouble by getting involved with him. The rules made sense. Ex-addicts had enough problems of their own, without taking on those of another ex-addict.

Slowly the staff members saw what was happening, but no one got as upset as we feared. Don Wilkerson occasionally even allowed us to go out together in the evening for a pizza, but he was always anxiously watching the clock when we returned. I loved him for bending the rules just a little and for trusting us that far. Once or twice we were even permitted to go out on double dates with my old counselor and friend, Sharon Webb, who was back in town and engaged to be married. Today I can laugh about having to ask permission to go out for an hour for a pizza at the ages of thirty-five and twenty-four, but at that time we took the guidance given us very seriously. We were not really totally grown up and responsible, and we knew it. We felt privileged to be trusted with any kind of dating at all and were determined to prove ourselves worthy of such faith.

However, the time came when word of our relationship got back to Dave Wilkerson. He was traveling a lot at that time and was at the center rather infrequently. But he kept his hand on the pulse of the whole organization. When he heard that Demi and I had been dating, he attacked the problem head-on in his customary fashion. "I want you and Cookie in my office at nine sharp tomorrow morning," was his abrupt invitation, issued to Demi one afternoon as they passed in the hall. We were left with one whole night to worry and wonder what was going to happen. Demi and I prayed together that night and again the next morning that Jesus would lead us in His own way. Then we joined Dave in the office.

At first he didn't speak directly to us but began praying for us aloud. "Thank You Lord, for Demi. Thank You for Cookie. Thank You and praise You for the great love You have for them and the mighty deliverance You have given them. Continue to bless them and protect them. Amen!"

Then he turned that piercing gaze of his directly at me and asked bluntly, "Are you in love with Demi?"

That was the question I had been refusing to ask myself, and I was startled to hear my own voice responding, without much hesitation, "Yes." I was immediately appalled by my nerve and acutely embarrassed. I didn't dare look at Demi.

But Dave was looking at him with that same steady look and asking him, "Do you love Cookie?"

Demi was even quicker to reply than I had been. "Yes I do!"

And so we discovered that we were in love. But Dave was not finished. "If Demi gave you an engagement ring, would you accept it?"

Oh, Lord, I'd never dared think that far—but my answer, as I darted a quick glance Demi's way, was again a very quiet, "Yes."

"Would you like to give Cookie an engagement ring?"

"*Yes!*" Demi almost shouted his response, and we all began to laugh.

I guess we really got engaged right on the spot. Dave gave Demi twenty-five dollars for a down payment on a ring and then later signed for him to buy the ring on credit. Trust Dave Wilkerson to clarify all issues by the direct approach.

Chapter 24

A UNION OF THREE

Dave Wilkerson had greater confidence in Demi and me than we had in ourselves at first. He reasoned that if two ex-junkies had any chance together at all, they would have a chance through the power and love of Jesus. He was therefore willing to trust the Lord with the details of our future together.

However, we were immediately tossed on waves of indecision by the advice we began getting from all sides.

"Get married right away to avoid temptation."

"You're crazy to consider marriage at all—it'll never work!"

"Wait awhile to marry so you can be really *sure!*"

Most of this advice was coming from other Christians whom we admired and respected. Which one was right? I found myself torn and confused all the time. I knew I loved Demi more than I'd ever thought I could possibly love a man, but did Jesus have marriage in mind for me? How could I ever be sure?

Nina was not so indecisive. She was absolutely certain that marriage to Demi was the best thing that could happen to her Irmita. She couldn't understand what he saw in me, but she was very impressed with his maturity, nice manners, and obvious affection for Dondi. She was among the minority who told me to marry him right away, before he changed his mind about me.

I must have given Demi his ring back three or four times during the remainder of that summer. I was upset by anyone's referring to my future plans, and concluded that such sensitivity and vacillation must indicate that I wasn't quite ready for marriage. Demi and I agreed to wait for a time.

Meanwhile I had been accepted at a college in Minneapolis. I planned to study Christian Education. This looked like a good way to begin working with young people, and I was thrilled that I had been accepted on the strength of my incomplete high-school record and my grades at Bible school. However, Dondi was still recuperating in the hospital and Demi, of course, planned to continue his work as a counselor at Teen Challenge. Going to college meant leaving behind the two persons I loved most in the world. I wasn't at all sure I was doing the right thing—but I sent in the advance deposit on my tuition and arranged a long series of meetings in churches throughout the Midwest to earn money for my tuition and expenses.

I had seen Dave only a few times since he'd gotten Demi and me engaged; but I bumped into him the day before my departure for the Midwest. I was upset to learn that he didn't think I should go. He asked me the questions I didn't want to answer: "What about Dondi? What about Demi? Are you sure you aren't just thinking about Cookie by going off to school now? For what shall it profit a woman if she shall gain the whole world and lose her own son?"

I recognized his deliberate misquote of Mark 8:36 and got the message. It *did* appear that I was running away from responsibility and decision. By that time I could no longer tell when my motives were good and when they were merely self-serving. I hated to disregard Dave's advice and counsel, but I saw no way to back out of my speaking engagements. As I packed for the trip no one, not even Demi, tried further to stop me.

During the three weeks that I was on tour, I got a good taste of the life of a traveling evangelist. I also got a good taste of homesickness and exhaustion—both physical and spiritual. Running from town to town and from meeting to meeting left me too little time for my personal prayer life and Bible study.

When I wasn't talking to one group or another I was talking long distance to Demi. My excuse was that I wanted to check on Dondi's progress; but actually I just wanted to talk with Demi about us and about our future together. The idea of spending a year away in college was becoming less and less attractive.

On the last night of my tour, I found myself dialing Dave Wilkerson's phone number. I needed a father's advice. When I had poured out all my frustrations and feelings of homesickness to him, he answered with, "Cookie, come on home. Forget about college for now. You'll always have a place somewhere in Teen Challenge. You have people here who need you—and it seems you need them, too. Come on home to Dondi and Demi."

I took his advice and the next bus headed for New York. My grueling schedule of speaking engagements had netted almost twelve hundred dollars—nearly enough for three years of Bible-school tuition. Since the money had been donated for the purpose of educating a Christian worker, I turned it over to Teen Challenge to be given to someone else who lacked the money to go on to school.

Despite Dave's assurance that Teen Challenge could be my home, there was just no room for me anywhere when I first got back to Clinton Avenue. Until a place could be found for me, I went to the Bronx to spend a little time with Nina and Dondi. He was out of the hospital at last and was sprinting around in a leg cast.

I couldn't believe how much I'd forgotten about tenement life in the year and a half I'd been living away from the ghetto. I felt like a stranger there. Those new eyes and ears the Lord had given me were appalled by what they saw and heard at Nina's apartment.

Loud cursing constantly filtered through the paper-thin walls, and the Lord's name was spoken only in vain. From sunrise until the small hours of the morning, loud record players blared tuneless noise. Dirty children ran shouting and crying through the building or played without supervision in the street. And the drunks! They were either storming around bellowing threats and insults at their families or else lying on the stairs in an alcoholic stupor. Since it was September and still warm outside, the apartment was always hot and humid, and foul odors permeated the close quarters.

The whole depressing scene drove me to my knees in prayer that the Lord would continue to send His people into the ghettos, to bring forth new life where there seemed to be no life at all. I knew that Dondi shouldn't remain in such an environment—but I saw no way of getting him out of it.

Eventually a position was made for me in the Teen Challenge office. I had hoped to be a counselor again—but I gratefully accepted any job that made it possible for me to return to the center. I was thankful for the rudimentary typing and filing skills that my aborted studies in a commercial high school had given me. Although the job was not exciting, it left my evenings free for informal street ministering and, as often as possible, some time with Demi.

That fall I finally discovered what it means to feel like a woman. I had felt loved by Jesus ever since He spoke to me at Rhinebeck—but now I experienced the joy of being loved by a flesh-and-blood man. I was warmed by Demi's faith in me and his acceptance of my past—an acceptance made more difficult for him by the constant reminders of those dreadful years that we encountered as we ministered in the ghetto. But Demi tried never to delve into the past or look for trouble. I loved him for ignoring all that had been, and also for his good judgment, his balanced outlook on life, and his great sense of humor. He was like a tonic to me. I just couldn't be depressed or sad around him. Best of all, I knew he loved Dondi like a son. He would make a wonderful father—strong, yet tender too. Nina was right: I was a lucky girl to have a man like him wanting me for his wife.

Still we were unable to bring ourselves to set a date for the wedding. The conflicting advice we were still getting made it difficult for us to take definite steps toward planning our future together.

Again it was Dave Wilkerson who came to our assistance. This time he spoke to us indirectly through a sermon the Lord must have given him just for us. It was about hearing and heeding the voice of the Lord. Dave said we all face times when outward circumstances are confusing and when the advice we receive conflicts with what we ourselves feel to be the right course of action. At such times, Dave cautioned, we have to go along with what God is telling us in our heart. "Weigh all the evidence; listen to all the advice; and then go with God's leading, not the world's." That message gave Demi and me the courage to go ahead with our plans for marriage. In our hearts, we felt that Jesus had given us our love for each other. Surely we could trust Him to honor our marriage with His continued blessing.

Demi and I were married on December 10, 1966, in the church his parents attended in Manhattan. All of Demi's family and mine, as well as the entire Teen Challenge staff, were invited to witness the ceremony. Sharon, who had just married her Richard, agreed to be my matron of honor, and Demi chose her husband as his best man. We had not forgotten those double dates the summer before.

December 10 was quite a day! I was the typical nervous bride as I dressed in the tiny (size three) beige dress that I had purchased with the last penny I owned. Richard came for me in his white car to take me to the church in style. Once I was carefully seated in the car, however, it refused to start. I struggled to hold back the tears as I said over and over, "I don't want to go to the church in the van."

Nevertheless, that's how I went to my wedding—in the seat of the same old van that we used for street rallies. I sat on the hard seat with clenched fists and a queasy stomach as we bumped and swayed our way along the city streets. My pride was more than a little wounded.

But once we arrived at the church, everything was set right again. The church was filled with love and a kind of gaiety. Dondi was there, all dressed up and fairly bouncing with excitement. Nina looked softer, almost tender, in the muted light of the church. And my joy was made complete by the unexpected presence of my mother, looking younger and prettier than ever. She was dressed so nicely and looked so pretty that many people mistook her for my sister in the course of the day. Seeing my family and Demi's together in the church, along with our Teen Challenge family, made me feel that the promise was being given for the blending of our two lives as one.

When we said our marriage vows, both Demi and I knew we were entering into a union of three, with Jesus very much a part of the merger. Since both of us were "in Christ," we were bound to each other in the love of Jesus, and the permanence of our vows was secured by no less a power than that of the Lord Himself. No wonder we felt confident we'd remain one until death!

After the ceremony, a reception was held at the church. Many of the guests pressed envelopes into our hands as they went down the receiving line—envelopes containing their good wishes and enough money to give us a weekend honeymoon in Pennsylvania. We began our married life with $200 in cash and no other earthly treasure except each other.

But Jesus gave me the best wedding present of all—one that only He could have given me. I had faced marriage that day with my past still troubling me. Demi seemed willing to forget what I'd done out in the streets to support my habit, and he never pressed me for any details about my old life. But I came to marriage still regretting that I wasn't a virgin. More than that, I was afraid that, after so much sexual abuse, I could not respond normally to a husband. The thought of giving my body to a man—even a loving man—was still abhorrent to me.

But I was reckoning without Jesus—without His power that makes all things new. On my wedding night I discovered that I felt like the most innocent of brides; that He had made me capable of a deep, loving relationship as a wife to Demi. Jesus' love had erased the memories and the fears. That night I became a woman who had no past—only a wonderful future as Mrs. Demi Rodriguez.

Chapter 25

ALL THE GOOD THINGS

A blow-by-blow account of the first months of any marriage is not necessary to make the point that adjustment is hard work. With our troubled backgrounds, Demi and I were bound to have a stormier adjustment than most couples—and we did.

For the first few weeks after we were married, we lived a rather disordered existence, traveling around a great deal as the front-line public relations team for the rallies Dave Wilkerson was then holding throughout the state of New York.

Demi and I prepared the way for the crusade team by going ahead to towns where rallies were scheduled and talking with church leaders and congregations about Teen Challenge. We both enjoyed being part of a direct people-to-people ministry and felt blessed to be able to cooperate in this way with the Holy Spirit as He prepared people for receiving the Good News.

However, this work had a hidden drawback that began to affect Demi quite adversely. In addition to being the advance workers for a rally, we often gave our testimonies during the actual meetings. There were several fellows on the crusade team who had been junkies, but I remained the lone female ex-addict on the staff. Dave was proud of me—of what Jesus had done through Teen Challenge in claiming my life for Himself. Dave also believed in frank, explicit talk when addressing a crowd at a rally. He was never one to mince words or to whitewash the truth. Therefore his introduction of me often went something like this:

I want you to meet Cookie. There she is over there, looking very pretty. She didn't look like that when I first met her. She was scrawny and miserable and mean as can be. I'd never seen anything so filthy unless it was a stray alley cat—and that's just about the dirtiest thing you can find!

He could go on and on with such graphic descriptions of my appearance and life style before I'd met the Lord. I never minded hearing what I was like then, because I knew he wasn't talking about me—about the person I had become. He was talking about some stranger who didn't know Jesus.

But I had never considered how Demi might feel. I never saw the hurt on his face as Dave talked that way about me. One day he could take it no longer and approached Dave right after a meeting. "Look, Dave," he began, "I know that you mean well, that you want to reach these people with the hard facts about drug addiction and life on the ghetto streets, but I can't stand hearing you talk about my wife like that. I know she had it tough, but that's all over now. I love the woman she is now and I can't stand to hear about the misery of her past. If this has to be part of our work with you, I'm afraid we won't be able to travel with you any more."

I couldn't believe I was hearing him correctly! But Dave understood at once and prayed with us right on the spot. Then he decided that we should return to the center in Brooklyn. I was a little slower to comprehend the problem, but gradually I realized that it was because of Demi's love for me that he couldn't bear to hear about the time when I was alone and unloved. He had accepted my past when he accepted me, but he didn't want to have to wallow in the sordid details. He was wise in letting Dave know how he felt, and I began to appreciate the feeling of being cherished and protected by my husband.

Back at Clinton Avenue, however, I was the one who had a problem! Demi was put to work as a counselor and soon became an assistant dean. He felt called upon to spend long, hard, hours with the boys who were going through the program. This made him less available to me. Since married women were not permitted to work as counselors, I returned to my job in the office. I began to resent the fact that Demi and I had so little time together, and also became very conscious of the attention that was centered on us as a couple of newlyweds. I had a lot to learn about living with a man, and the small room that was our home at the center gave me very little of the privacy I craved during this learning period.

Perhaps Demi and I at first relied *too* much on the Lord to make our marriage work and failed to realize that He expected some cooperation and effort from us. We needed to invest more of ourselves in our marriage—but we seldom seemed to have the time and privacy to do so.

Another difficulty, I'm sure, was the fact that I had absolutely no concept of what made a marriage a good one, since my childhood was so completely lacking in models to copy. I didn't know a single thing about men that was useful or helpful in adjusting to my new role as a wife. I rather thought that Demi and I would always be happy, friendly, warm, loving, and completely cooperative in all things. In no time at all after our honeymoon, however, I discovered that Demi had a lot of flaws I'd never noticed before. On a day-in, day-out basis, he wasn't "Mr. Perfect" after all. And naturally on closer scrutiny I didn't look so great to him either. Many of my faults and problems became all too apparent.

None of these adjustment problems would have been a surprise to a couple better equipped for marriage, and they could have been dealt with a lot more readily had we not been living in such close proximity to the Christian people we worked with every day— all of whom had, if anything, *too* much interest in seeing our marriage succeed. How could two fiery Latin tempers do justice to a disagreement if we thought others would hear us quarreling? I was secretly afraid that such arguments weren't normal either—that they meant we weren't living the kind of life Jesus wanted for us.

Clearly we needed some time to learn about loving, about surrendering our egos in love, and about seeking forgiveness and giving it freely. We needed greater privacy. We needed to get away from those who knew us too well. At the center we were almost public property—display case items.

Since we both felt the strain, Demi jumped at the chance to go to a new Teen Challenge rehabilitation program that was opening up in Saint Louis. It needed experienced staff members, and *we* needed to get away from the Brooklyn Center. It seemed the ideal solution.

Almost as soon as we were settled in Saint Louis, I became aware that I was pregnant. In the middle of our first crusade I became lightheaded and then actively sick—a most uncomfortable and embarrassing experience. But despite continuing morning sickness, I was as delighted as Demi that the Lord was blessing our union so promptly with a child. As we made excited plans for this baby, our thoughts turned more and more to another child. Dondi was still living with Nina in New York.

Leaving him to go to Saint Louis had not been easy for either of us. Nina had allowed him to visit with us at the Brooklyn center on weekends, but she would not talk of our keeping him permanently. Neither of us wanted to hurt her by insisting on my rights as Dondi's mother. We knew that her feelings were based on her attachment to him, and not on any real anxiety about our ability to love and care for him. She had taken Dondi as a puny premature infant, whom I could not have cared for, and had raised him these seven years to be the healthy, happy child he was. He was the apple of her eye, and giving him up would be very painful for her.

But we loved him too, and Demi wanted very much to adopt him as his own son. We began to pray earnestly that the Lord would work out this whole problem without hurting Nina any further. As if in answer to that prayer, she allowed Dondi to visit us in Saint Louis that summer. He seemed so happy with us that we became more and more reluctant to send him back to live in the ghetto again.

As we considered our hopes for Dondi, we had to face certain practical matters that we hadn't thought about before. In order to prove himself fit to be an adoptive father, Demi would have to demonstrate stability, as well as the ability to support a family. An ex-addict is never regarded highly as a potential adoptive parent; and since we were *both* ex-addicts, we knew that our qualifications would receive particularly intensive scrutiny.

At that time, Teen Challenge had not received the national recognition and support that it enjoys today.

The entire ministry was operated by faith on a day-to-day basis. As need for money arose, Dave Wilkerson and those associated with him prayed and trusted the Lord to provide. This was truly inspiring work. Time and again the Lord blessed our faith and provided what was needed at just the perfect moment.

A faith ministry, however, is somewhat hard to explain to uncommitted persons. In practical terms Demi could not claim a steady income of more than fifteen dollars a week. We began to realize that this kind of life would not be likely to impress the authorities with our stability. What did the Lord want us to do? Surely He didn't want us to desert His work just to prove something to the world!

As we prayed and asked His leading, however, we became increasingly convinced that He did indeed have "civilian life" in mind for us. We decided to join our friends, Sharon and David, in the town of Columbus, Ohio, where they had settled. They found us an apartment and helped Demi secure employment as a mechanic. With mixed emotions, we left the Teen Challenge ministry and headed for Columbus to become average citizens, if we could.

Just before we left Saint Louis, we saw the second step of the Lord's answer to our prayers for Dondi. Nina called to tell us that, because the school teachers were on strike in New York City, she felt we ought to take Dondi with us to Columbus. Nothing could have pleased us more. And so the three of us settled down to a totally new way of living in a community far removed—geographically and in other respects—from the Bronx ghetto.

At first we had frequent moments of doubt, wondering if we had truly followed the leading of Jesus or our own selfish desires. But as we gradually became a part of the community, the Lord began to

177

bless our lives in many diverse ways. First He gave us a second son, Danny, born in November. Then Nina called to tell us she wanted us to keep Dondi as our own. The Lord had put the idea into her heart without our ever having to ask her about it. How we praised Him for His wisdom and compassion!

Finally He began to bless us also "in the marketplace." Demi was making a fine salary, and I too was able to enter the business world when a neighbor stepped forward to volunteer help with baby-sitting. For Demi and me to find that we could hold steady jobs proved important to both of us.

In the spring of 1969, Demi legally adopted Dondi as his son. By that time we had been living in Columbus for a year and a half. Before another year had passed, we had a three-bedroom brick home of our own, wall-to-wall carpeting, two cars, and three children! Our Crissy was born on our third anniversary—December 10, 1969. She was the Lord's answer to our prayer for a little girl.

Our lives at that point seemed filled to capacity with all the good things a couple of ex-junkies could ever want. We were surrounded by the love of God, Who had given us a beautiful family, a lovely home, and a sense of peace and security in a world that had once seemed ugly and confusing. Our marital adjustments had been satisfactorily made, and we were blissfully happy with each other and with our lot in life. We would still be in Columbus today if the Lord had not begun to show us that He had other plans for us.

Chapter 26

BLIND STEPS IN FAITH

Even today I marvel that the Lord was able to call us away from the security of Columbus into a future that contained many uncertainties, many blind steps in faith. How did He do it? How did He persuade us to give up our very pleasant life as average middle-class American parents—a life He had so richly blessed?

The answer was partly in the fact that Jesus remained Lord of our lives while we were living in Columbus. It was He Who had led us there, and He had blessed our lives there with a sense of His presence in addition to many of the good things of this world. He had never ceased to be our strength and our guide for living. Therefore we continued to expect His leading and we continued to seek His will.

Circumstances also contributed to our willingness to move when He called. One of the few disturbing aspects of life in Columbus had been our decision to conceal our past from our new friends and neighbors. We wanted to be accepted for ourselves, to be treated like everyone else—and we felt this acceptance would be impossible if our past histories were known. In a way this was a wise decision, because too many people who knew about our lives B.C. gave us too much credit and forgot Who was the author of our new lives.

But the decision to conceal our past caused unforeseen difficulties. When I filled out a job application, for example, I was faced with questions about drugs. I didn't actually lie, but I didn't tell the *whole* truth. Even at the time, I knew I was not living up to the Lord's standard. Then came a time when I had to refuse an invitation to be a "block parent" because of my police record. Dondi was *so* disappointed—but I couldn't face delving into all of that just to serve the community in such a minor way.

Eventually we did discover a kind of release in sharing our histories with certain close friends in Columbus. We weren't really ashamed of our past, but neither were we using our uniqueness to glorify God. This kind of compromise made us feel that we were not fully cooperating with our God. He let us struggle with this problem until He needed us for His plans. Then He used the uneasiness we already felt to call us gently out of the life we were leading.

About the time Crissy was born, the news media began to carry more and more depressing stories about the rising rate of drug addiction in New York City and other urban areas. The statistics quoted in these stories also indicated that drugs were getting into the suburbs and rural areas, and to younger and younger age groups. We began to feel somehow that we were just sitting around in our ivory tower when we should have been out there doing battle on the front line.

I recall very well the evening we were watching a TV special on drug addiction. The participants told the story of a twelve-year-old boy who had died in New York of a heroin overdose. Twelve years old! Our Dondi would be turning ten that summer, and twelve was not far away. As bad as my own past had been, I was still appalled and sickened that such young children were being wasted.

The calling I had received from Jesus nearly 5½ years earlier began to haunt me. What was I doing to help the young people He had given me as a burden? I tried hard to excuse myself. After all, I was busy being a wife and mother. But somehow there was no real comfort in that explanation.

Demi was even more distressed and moved by that television program than I had been. He asked me to join him in prayer about what we had seen and heard. As we asked the Lord to do something about those children—all the lost ones in the ghetto—I suddenly *knew* that our vacation from the active ministry of Jesus Christ was over. He had given us the time we needed to make our marriage strong and to lay the foundations of our family. Now it seemed He was calling us back to His full-time service.

At nine the next Monday morning Demi called the center and talked to Don Wilkerson. Then he flew to New York to have a personal interview with Don and to look over the program as it had developed since our departure three years earlier.

When he returned, we knew that we were facing a major decision. We had three children to support. We also had a house with a mortgage, but we had no other debts. Demi's salary was more than sufficient to meet our needs. I had stopped working when Chrissy was born, and was devoting myself full time to raising my family and making a home for Demi. This life represented the most financial and emotional security either of us had ever known. Were we foolish to consider trading it all for a life in the center in Brooklyn—for fifteen dollars a week, a crowded apartment, and the uncertainties of a faith ministry? Demi did ask for my opinion, but I could see that he'd already made the decision. We put the house up for sale, and I began to pack.

Strangely enough, a very attractive opportunity to remain in Columbus was presented to us about that time. A lay Catholic group offered Demi a chance to begin a program right in Columbus. The offer was very tempting, and we thought that perhaps the Lord was not going to ask us to give up the pleasant life we'd been enjoying as private citizens, or our pretty little house. As we prayed about the offer, however, we felt that it was not what the Lord was calling us to. Again the decision was ultimately Demi's; but I knew he was right to turn it down. I was in accord with his decision to return to Brooklyn.

We arrived at the Clinton Avenue building on June 5, 1970. Demi was again hired as a counselor. Since I was not only married but was also the mother of three young children, I fully expected to be put on a shelf or used in a minor supporting role in the program. But I was wrong. Don Wilkerson called me in shortly after our return and told me that they would find a baby-sitter for me if I would agree to direct the summer evangelism program that year. So I became the first woman ever to direct street evangelism for Teen Challenge. Attitudes toward women, and particularly those who were ex-addicts, certainly seemed to be changing in the center. I accepted the leadership position very eagerly.

This change in attitude was not the only difference we found on returning to the center. We discovered Teen Challenge's financial situation had also changed quite significantly. We were still not going to acquire great wealth in this ministry; but the salaries had increased greatly and were almost regular by then.

Dave Wilkerson's widely acclaimed book, *The Cross and the Switchblade,* had focused the nation's attention upon the Lord's work in the ghetto and among drug addicts. The support of a large population of His people had been the gratifying result.

We were not going to be destitute in this ministry after all. We had a tiny but adequate apartment, and we were putting our unique backgrounds to work for our Lord. We found ourselves no less content in Brooklyn than we had been in Columbus.

I loved the part the Lord gave me that summer. Along with holding the regular street meetings, I initiated some night rallies that really attracted the crowds. Junkies are night people by nature, and the heat of those summer evenings brought everyone out of the sweltering tenements to clap hands to our Gospel music. As often as I could, I asked my favorite preacher to accompany me at these night rallies; but when Demi couldn't make it, there were always others ready to share the Good News at any time.

I never tired of these meetings. I was always thrilled to see the quiet—the real sense of peace—that fell upon the ragtag crowds who at first were hooting and catcalling. The quieting effect of the Holy Spirit on such gatherings was truly miraculous. I saw many lives being touched.

One person that Jesus touched that summer was Frances. I first met her on a street in the Bronx among a group of addicts we approached on a hot summer night. Frances stayed at the back of the group with head hanging. For some reason, she reminded me of myself when I was out on the streets and all strung out. I made a special effort to speak to her, and when we left I told her I'd return the next day to talk with her some more. I was surprised to find her waiting eagerly for me when I fulfilled my promise. She represented all that was wrong with girls in the street, and yet—to our amazement—she seemed very responsive to the moving of the Spirit in her life.

Even Demi, as removed from the street ministry to girls as he was at that time, was touched by the eagerness with which Frances received the Word of God. On days when I had no plan to visit the Bronx, he'd surprise me by suggesting that we go see Frances. I didn't know it then, but meeting Frances had given Demi his first real burden for girls.

Knowing Frances also began to bring home to us the inadequacies of our efforts to help the hard-core addicts. We were reaching out to hundreds of afflicted persons, but we were able to provide only a handful of places for them to go for rehabilitation.

All too often, the spark of hope kindled in the eyes of a junky by our testimony to the saving power of Jesus would burn out before a place became available in the rehabilitation program. The girls' programs were the tightest. The Teen Challenge ministry to girls was continuing in Garrison, New York, with John Benton still in charge; but the number of girls they could handle at any one time was pathetically inadequate. A girl had to wait months for a place, and then was admitted to the program only if she could pass rather stringent admission requirements. In light of the shortage of available places, it was only sensible to take the most promising girls; but I was saddened by the realization that *I* would not have qualified under the standards that were now being applied.

I wondered how many more girls like me were being screened out and never given a chance for rehabilitation. Even one would have been too many, and I knew there were many, many more than one.

That summer, as I watched Frances waiting and waiting for the same chance the Lord had given me, my burden for the girls in the street grew heavy. Step by step, the Lord was preparing me for a new kind of ministry.

Chapter 27

A CALL TO MINISTER

I knew I was pregnant again when the nausea started. With each pregnancy I had experienced some degree of morning sickness, but this time I was practically incapacitated. My unpredictable bouts of prostration put an end to my work in the street ministry. I did a little baby-sitting for staff members, but otherwise lapsed into total uselessness.

One thing I could do, and suddenly had more time to do than ever before, was *pray*. The girls out in the street, who were my special burden, received the greatest of my efforts. I persistently asked the Lord to open a way for them to get the help they needed. I had no idea that He might want to answer this prayer through me.

As I approached the fourth month of pregnancy and began feeling almost normal again, I was bothered by the recurring idea that the Lord wanted me to begin a jail ministry. I couldn't understand the persistence of this notion, since I knew how long Teen Challenge had been trying in vain to get into the city jails. One night as I was praying I was astonished to receive a vision of the miserable old women's house of detention in Greenwich Village. I wondered what on earth the Lord was trying to tell me. That was surely the last place on earth where I'd be allowed to minister! I'd been an inmate there myself eight different times in the past. But as I continued to pray the vision returned, and I felt that I was being called to a ministry there.

"Now Jesus," I argued, "You know how Demi feels about my working when I'm pregnant. If You want me to go there now, You'll have to deal with him. And then what are we going to do with the girls we minister to when they get out? The girls' programs can't handle any more, You know. How do You plan to talk the Teen Challenge directors into approving such a scheme?"

He didn't give me the answers to those questions, but He kept laying on my heart the burden for ministering to the inmates of that jail. Finally I knew I'd just have to try to follow His lead, and leave the rest up to Him. However, I couldn't resist challenging Him one last time. "OK, Lord," I said, "have it Your way. I'll try to get such a plan approved, but You'll have to get Don Wilkerson and John Benton together so I can talk to both of them about this. They are the ones who will have to give me the green light."

Nothing like asking for the impossible! Since he moved to Garrison with the girl's program, John Benton was seldom seen at Clinton Avenue. Nevertheless as I approached Don Wilkerson's office that morning and asked to see him, his secretary nodded and said, "You're in luck, Cookie. He's still in there with Brother Benton."

I never considered the impropriety of just barging into the office. When I saw how fast Jesus was answering my prayers, I was too excited to think clearly. I had to share with these two men what the Lord had been telling me before I burst. To my surprise, they both endorsed the idea without much hesitation. Don said, "If the Lord is leading, go ahead and try for a pass."

My heart sank. They'd never let me in with my record! However, Don dictated a beautiful letter for me to use as a reference when I asked for a pass. In it he described me as a rehabilitated drug addict.

The last obstacle was Demi. He was out of town again, but he called me that night. As I shared with him all that happened in the past twenty-four hours, he grew more and more enthusiastic. "If it's the Lord leading you, Cookie, go ahead and do it!" Again I had reason to thank God for the husband He had given me, and for his trust in me as well as in the Lord. He had been the easiest to convince of them all.

Now the only hurdle that remained was to secure a pass to visit the House of Detention. By this time I should have realized that the Lord was truly in this ministry and that He was going to take care of that detail too. I was so fired up with enthusiasm, however, that I decided to give Him a little help. The letter that Don had dictated for me didn't look so good when I studied it closely. Why was it necessary to tell the prison authorities I was an ex-addict? I didn't think they'd mind that I was a rehabilitated gang member—but the drug part might queer the deal. I decided to dictate a new letter with that fact omitted.

As I sat in the office of the Department of Corrections, watching the face of the officer who was reading my letter, I wondered what on earth had possessed me to tamper with Don's original letter of introduction. I became so uneasy that I finally went over to the officer and told him that I had also been an addict. His expression hardly changed as he asked, "How long ago was that?" I had to think a minute before I realized that it had been almost seven years since I'd had my last fix. Seven years! Could that be correct? The officer just smiled and said, "Well, then you are legally defined as a 'cured addict'—a mighty rare creature from what I hear. Don't you know that the state legislature passed a five-year survival figure a few years ago? Congratulations! I've never known a girl who made it!" And the next thing I knew I had a pass in my hands. I was officially cured. My past didn't really matter to the prison officials at all. The legal definition of a cure had been passed while Demi and I were living in Columbus. Finding out about it was a big bonus to the success I was feeling in following the Lord into a new jail ministry.

Everything had gone so smoothly that I began to expect the red-carpet treatment all the way. With my social agency pass in hand, I confidently paid my first visit to jail itself. And there I was stopped cold. "We already have too many people coming in here to visit these girls," the matron said. "I'm sorry, but we cannot accept you." I couldn't believe my ears. After opening all those doors, surely the Lord did not intend to close this one!

I guess He wanted me to have some part in the miracle He was performing, because I found myself frantically sharing my story and my burden for the girls in that prison with the cold, stern-faced matron. I watched as she began to look interested, then asked me some questions, and finally relented to the point of allowing me one girl to visit for two hours once a week.

The first Monday in January was the day the jail ministry officially began. Lois was my first "client." We were given a small corner in the social-service department as an "office." Whatever I wanted to do with her—whether to talk, advise, pray, or just listen— had to be done in full view and earshot of everyone in the department. Concentration was all but impossible.

Nevertheless, Lois returned the 'next week and the next. The third time she brought a friend. Colleen was a large, defiant-appearing girl who managed to send an icy shudder through me the first time she sized up my tiny frame with her cold, black eyes. I started to pray silently the minute I saw her that Jesus would give me the love and patience I would need to minister to such a forbidding-looking girl. Then she began to tell us why she had come.

She had decided to come and see me because she had heard all the "lies" I'd been telling Lois. She thought I must be crazy. At once she began to challenge me with an aggressive attack on my teaching. "I hear you used to be on drugs and into stealing and prostitution," she sneered. "And that Jesus came into your life and all of a sudden you didn't want drugs again." Disbelief was oozing from every word as she talked. "Well, listen! I been on drugs heavy for five years, and I know there is no way out!"

Then she outlined the holdup and murder for which she had been sent to jail. She and her crime partner had not meant to hurt anyone—they were after money—but the grocer they were robbing had pulled a knife on Colleen and she had shot him. Her partner, who was also her "old man," had fled—leaving her to take the rap alone. She was clearly more distressed at being deserted by her old man than she was at having killed a man. As she spat out each fact of her past, I could see in her haunted expression the abject loneliness that told the real story.

"I'm alone now," she said defiantly, "and I've promised myself I'll never rely on anyone ever again. From now on I make it on my own."

I watched the hurt and anger alternating in those cold eyes. Then I prayed silently, "Jesus, I know that an innocent man is dead today because of Colleen.

190

But, Jesus, she's lost and confused and very much alone. She needs You. Give me the words to help her to know You."

Then it was my turn to talk—to share my past. I told them of the hurts I'd had and the way I'd blamed everything wrong in my life on someone else —my parents who didn't want me, my grandmother who didn't understand me, the kids at school who didn't accept me. And I told her how Jesus had come to me in a crowded auditorium one night and showed me personally that He loved me and had died for me centuries earlier. I told her how He had given me tears of repentance. When I had finished speaking, Colleen was sobbing and confessing, "I been so lonely, Cookie! All my life I been lonely. Oh, Cookie, I need Jesus! How do I tell Him I need Him?"

As I led her through prayer to the presence of Jesus, I was crying—and Lois was crying, too. It was a new beginning for Colleen, and for many other girls who would be touched by her changed life. Our group soon contained more girls who wanted to hear about what had made Colleen so different all of a sudden.

Eventually Colleen was sentenced to seven years in the upstate penitentiary, but even this tough sentence did not lessen her testimony. The day after she was sentenced, she shared her thoughts with the largest group that had ever gathered with me in jail. "Girls, I've learned that my real jail was inside me—in my heart. All my friends on the outside of these prison walls aren't free like I am now that Jesus has set me free." And that day many of the hardest girls in the prison wept at her testimony and gave their hearts to the Lord.

Shortly after Colleen left to serve her sentence, the House of Detention was moved to a new location on

Riker's Island. When I first heard about the new building, I boldly asked for more space and more days to visit. But when the new jail was opened I had to make do with visits through the glass partition at the visitors' room. Prayer and counseling had to be done over a telephone. Still the Lord continued to bless the ministry He had begun.

He also blessed the Rodriguez family with another little girl. Geniece was born conveniently on a Tuesday. I was at the jail for my weekly session with the girls the day before her birth, and the next Monday I was back again.

Finally the chaplain took pity on us and offered his small study for a Bible-study group. As more and more girls crowded into our meetings, the warden finally assigned an office and two classrooms for this ministry. The work of the Spirit was very much in evidence. Not only were girls meeting Jesus as Savior; some were also being baptized in the Spirit. They, in turn, were starting prayer circles at night in their cells. At one time, eighteen prayer circles were in operation. Surely no one but God could have inspired such behavior in a jail!

I had many occasions to thank God for the fact that the jail ministry was His and not mine. I would not have survived one day in that work if I had not been absolutely certain that He was going to lead in each situation and deal with each problem as it arose. I needed His strength and protection as well as His guidance.

Constant exposure to "hopelessness" occasionally caused a sort of contagious hopelessness in my own spirit. Once I'd gained the confidence of the girls, I was often called to be a kind of confessor. They told me things that they would never admit in court. One day, after hearing a particularly depressing story from a very hardened young woman, I found myself feeling so oppressed and upset that I could hardly function. Eventually the combined prayers of the Teen Challenge staff, with laying on of hands, were needed to restore me to normalcy and balance again.

Thereafter when I discovered that I was unusually oppressed by a particular girl or her history, I always sought prayer from other Christians. Usually I found I was trying to deal with the girl's sin in my own strength and not in the Lord's. Prayer set things right once again.

Every day of the jail ministry became an adventure in faith and an opportunity for me to observe the Lord's work at close hand. I was grateful to be used in this ministry, but was thankful that I could leave the results in His hands.

Chapter 28

FRUSTRATION

Soon the jail ministry was bearing fruit that could not be contained behind prison walls. As girls became eligible for parole or release, I often found myself serving in the unaccustomed roles of lawyer and social worker. Occasionally a girl would be released on my assurance that she would immediately enter a rehabilitation program. And there was the problem! The girls' home was far too small to handle the growing number of converted female addicts who needed the help of caring Christians as they made their way back from the streets.

I felt alone in my frustration over the inadequacy of the Christian rehabilitation centers for women. Even Demi, although he supported my work in the women's prison with prayer and advice, could not understand why I got so upset with the situation. He tried using logic on me: "Honey, you've got to understand that not every girl who's in jail today can get into a rehabilitation home. A lot of them don't want to, and a lot more would never be able to stand it there. You've got to learn to be happy with what is possible and not get bogged down with the things that won't change with worry. You're doing a great job with those girls. Just thank God for all He is accomplishing through your ministry."

I did thank God for that. And I appreciated the

truth of Demi's reasoning. I tried to cast my discontent on the Lord, figuring that He could handle it far better than I. But my burden for women addicts grew and grew. I knew from personal experience that they need *special* help. More time, more patience, more love, and more prayer are required for them than for the male addict, because they have more personal hurt to hand over to Jesus. It takes a girl longer to realize that Jesus forgives *all* sin, that forgiveness is forever, and that a new way of life doesn't depend upon her deserving it. My whole being cried out for those tortured girls who weren't getting the time and love they needed, and who consequently came back to the jails time and time again. I *knew* that vicious cycle, and I wanted so much for Jesus to break into the endless round of pain and punishment. How I prayed for the Lord to minister special caring to these girls who were society's saddest outcasts! Of course I knew He would respond to such a prayer: but when He did, it took me some time to understand His approach.

I went to court one day with a junkie named Rosita. She'd been caught stealing again, and I was standing in as counsel for her when the judge ruled that she could be released to the custody of Teen Challenge. I watched her expression of surprise give way to hope, then to unrestrained joy as she realized that, instead of another prison term, she was being given a real chance to get her life together. We hugged each other and cried and laughed together as we left the courtroom.

I could hardly wait to tell Demi. He knew how concerned I'd been for Rosita—how I'd prayed that Jesus would reach her before she had to serve more time. She had already reached that critical point where any further hardening would prove almost irreparable. One more prison term would have made reaching her much more difficult—but at this point she was willing to give Jesus a chance. How thankful I was that the court had given her the opportunity to find a new life!

I hurried her off to Clinton Avenue to see if any of the girls' homes could possibly take her. As usual, they were filled to capacity. Fortunately I had already warned Rosita of that possibility. We had discussed the idea of her going back to Puerto Rico to enter a rehabilitation program Teen Challenge was operating there, and she had agreed. All we needed was the seventy-dollar plane fare to get her on her way. Then I discovered that the Brooklyn Center could not even supply that need.

At first I heard the news in disbelief and anger. How could that be? We always seemed to have resources to handle an emergency. And this was an emergency! Rosita was our responsibility. She'd been paroled to our custody, and we had to find her a place. Slowly it sank in that no one was holding back any money. All the funds had simply been used elsewhere, and it would take time to replace them.

I figured time was exactly what Rosita did not have. Already she was looking edgy and distracted— exactly the way any addict looks as he thinks about finding a fix. She was sincere enough in desiring to try a rehabilitation program, but I knew that she might cut out at the first opportunity unless we got her on her way quickly.

I prayed fast and furiously. I didn't know where else to turn. Demi was out of town that day, and he couldn't have provided the money anyway. I prayed hard for some leading, and concluded that I would have to go begging.

Out on the streets of Brooklyn I went with Rosita in tow. We stood at the subway entrance, and I stopped every passer-by I could to ask for money to save this girl's life. The majority looked at me with eyes filled with contempt. I knew what they were thinking: "There's another addict whore begging money to get a fix!" After four hours, however, the Lord had sent enough generous persons. I bought Rosita's ticket and put her on the plane bound for Puerto Rico.

Shaking with fatigue, I began to think how easy it would be for Rosita, once in Puerto Rico, just to walk away without ever going to the Teen Challenge Center. I grew depressed. Had it been worth all the humiliation of begging just to get that plane ticket? Immediately I was ashamed. Of course it was worth it! What if Ruth Cowgill had asked the same question when I needed a bed my first night at Clinton Avenue? Nevertheless I knew all too well how strongly Rosita would be tempted, and I feared she would be sidetracked before the goal was reached.

When Demi finally returned home and I shared with him the events of the day, he was incredulous and upset. "You mean you actually went out on the streets and *begged* for the money to send her to Puerto Rico?" he asked, almost shouting. "What on earth were you thinking about? You might have gotten rolled yourself!"

I gave him time to ventilate his concern for my safety, because I knew what would follow. And sure enough, he was soon saying, "Honey, I'm proud of you—I really am. I know I couldn't have done what you did for any of these girls. I know *you* couldn't have done it either if Jesus hadn't been leading you. When I think about how long it took us to get Frances into a rehabilitation program this summer—and now there's this business of having to go begging for these girls. I think maybe the Lord is trying to tell us something. Maybe He wants us to do something ourselves to help the girls."

That night, out of our shared prayers and concern for the girls in the streets, was born the faint beginning of the fantastic new ministry the Lord had in store for Demi and me.

Chapter 29

A FARM IN PENNSYLVANIA

At first we had no idea how great was the size of the commitment Jesus was asking from us. He had first given me a burden for girls and then made sure that Demi was in accord; but it took time before we saw what He was unfolding in our lives.

Initially we were focusing too much attention upon the size of the women's program at Teen Challenge. Somehow we felt that all that was needed was more *room* for girls. If we could just somehow expand the ministry to girls, I felt we'd be meeting the need. The problem of placing girls had been so acute that I was thinking in terms of quantity rather than quality.

However, the *size* of the womens' ministry was not the whole problem. Something else was wrong. The girls were not responding to the rehabilitation programs in the same way that the fellows were. Despite a stringent screening process, far too many girls were leaving the programs prematurely. Among the staff workers, a feeling was growing that girls were too hard to reform. Many were beginning to believe that female junkies were beyond redemption.

Of course I couldn't agree. What about *me?* No one would ever have voted me the "girl most likely to succeed in a Christ-centered rehabilitation program," but the Lord had worked a miracle in me. I couldn't believe that He wanted to save a lot of male addicts and let all the girl junkies on the street go unredeemed. The Jesus I knew did not discriminate between the sexes.

Still, the statistics were depressing. They had not improved since the days when Rhinebeck was closed to make a Bible school. The girls' programs were losing too many of their members back to the streets. They were as expensive to operate as the boys' programs, but they were not bearing the same fruit. What were we doing wrong? A girl named Sylvia helped us answer the question.

One evening in May, 1972, we heard a timid knocking on our apartment door. We opened it to find Sylvia weeping on our threshold. "Oh, Cookie!" she sobbed. "Please help me! I want to live for Jesus now, but I need help! Please, Cookie! I can't do it without help!"

Sylvia was an unmarried junkie who had three little girls and another child on the way. I had thought she *was* getting help. Hadn't we sent her to a newly-opened rehabilitation center just the week before? Nethertheless I asked her to come in, and then we heard her story.

"Cookie, they didn't understand me where I was! They seemed to know what the guys needed, but they didn't dig me at all. I tried to tell them how I feel about my past, about my children, about being pregnant again—but I could see they didn't understand what it's really like. I got to feeling alone and empty—and I started thinking about drugs again. Oh, Cookie, you've been through all this. You can help me, can't you? Let me stay with you, let me clean your apartment or take care of your children for you—anything! Only please show me how you made it. I know I won't make it unless I get help."

We didn't have room for an extra person in that

apartment, but Demi's nod told me to get some sheets and bed her down on the sofa. She had come to us desperate for help. What did we have to offer her that we hadn't already tried?

I began to think about my own rehabilitation—begun at Clinton Avenue, continued at Rhinebeck, and brought nearer to completion in El Paso. The Lord wasn't done with me, of course—I am still in the process of growing in His wisdom and His love—but I had no doubt that He'd been the author of all the help I'd received along the way. Then why weren't the Christ-centered programs turning out many more women with new lives?

Suddenly I recalled how different I'd felt from all the people who had first ministered to me—how sure I was that the God of such "nice" folks would want nothing to do with the likes of me. I heard a similar note in Sylvia's cry for help. What she was really saying was, "I can believe in *your* Jesus, Cookie, because He brought you out of a drug-filled past as bad as mine, but I'm not so sure about the Jesus of those nice people who staff the girls' homes." This was a kind of reverse snobbery, of course, but one that I really understood.

Maybe the Lord had helped me survive in my own rehabilitation because He needed me to lead other girls like myself to a new life in Him. He'd given me just a taste of this work in the jail ministry He'd opened up for me. Now it appeared that He wanted me to see the girls through to their complete rehabilitation. Perhaps this was the reason I'd been spared from death in the streets, the reason I'd been baptized in His Spirit, the reason I'd been united with a mature Christian husband, and the reason we'd both been given a burden for girls. Everything seemed to be pointing to the possibility that Jesus wanted us to help Him lead girls—the really down-and-out kinds—to Him. And suddenly, I wanted very much to be a part of just such a ministry.

Demi and I at once began to discuss the possibility of forming a new ministry dealing exclusively with girls. We concluded that if Jesus wanted that from us, He could show us how and when and where.

Our first step of faith was to share our hopes with Don Wilkerson, who seemed to like our ideas and agreed that we should present this new ministry in all our speaking engagements. Soon we were sharing our dream of a separate ministry for girls with everyone we met. With encouraging frequency, our enthusiastic presentation met with answering enthusiasm.

Slowly, doors began to open. A church group from Pennyslvania came to Brooklyn to talk with Demi and me about our dream of a girls' ministry. They spoke of a fifty-five-acre farm we could use if it turned out to be suitable for us. Then Nicky Cruz called us about a new ministry he was starting in North Carolina. He needed a director, and he wanted to work with girls as well as boys in his center. We seemed suddenly to have a choice of two directions to pursue.

In June we were able to take some time off to look into both of these possibilities. We headed first for York, Pennsylvania, to look over the farm that had been offered to us. The whole idea of a farm setting for this ministry appealed to both Demi and me. Clean air, lots of trees and grass, and blue skies overhead seemed to us to be just what a girl needed as she began to live a new life. A drastic change in environment from the filthy ghetto would be a definite asset.

The farm lived up to our hopes. It was just beautiful! We could hardly believe our good fortune. The

Lord was being generous indeed to open the door to such a lovely home for our girls' ministry.

We also shared our dreams with the church congregation which had invited us to York. In the process we gained some new friends.

One of the members of the church who came forward to meet us was a gentle, lovely lady named Pauline Bernstein. Pauline had been a Christian until her marriage to a York businessman who was Jewish. Until the death of her husband, she had attended temple and raised her children in the Jewish faith. Then, shortly after being widowed, she had met Jesus in a new way and had rededicated her life to His service. She was warmly enthusiastic about our idea of a ministry just for girls and promised her support in whatever way we might need it. I loved her immediately for her motherly interest in us and for her obvious sincerity in wanting to help. Altogether, the trip to York seemed to have had results.

At that point it was hard even to consider North Carolina. "The Lord must want us in Pennsylvania," we reasoned. "Why else would He have given us a farm?" Nevertheless, we did travel to North Carolina to look over the new center there. Everything looked good except for the fact that we would be working with both male and female addicts. Another drawback was the distance from New York City. The burden I had been given was for girls in the city jails and on the ghetto streets. It seemed impractical to try to deal with them from as far away as North Carolina. As we prayed for guidance, we felt more and more certain that Jesus wanted us on a farm in Pennsylvania.

We returned to Brooklyn full of excitement and high hopes for beginning our ministry in short order. Sylvia had been staying with us off and on during this time. She was torn between life in the streets and life in the Lord, and it often appeared that the streets were winning. We felt sure that getting her on a farm and away from New York would help us win the battle for her life and soul.

We had just resigned from our positions at Teen Challenge when the bad news came. The farm that had been promised to us for a girls' ministry did not belong to the people who had made the offer. It wasn't theirs to give.

We were crushed and bewildered by this unexpected turn of events. We had felt so sure that the Lord was leading us to a farm in Pennsylvania. Had we misunderstood? Did He want us to go to North Carolina after all? We were beginning to feel a bit foolish as we remained at Teen Challenge waiting for the Lord to show us where He wanted us. We considered asking for our old jobs on the staff, but something held us back. In spite of these setbacks, we felt that Jesus was calling us to minister to girls, and that we had to trust Him to show us, in His own time, where it was to be.

One day Pauline Bernstein called us with the news that she had found a ten-acre farm for sale. We dashed out to York to take a look. The land was lovely, but there were no habitable buildings on the property. No buildings meant no program for several months at least, and we didn't feel the Lord wanted us to wait so long to get to work. It was just another false lead. Both of us were very quiet on the way back to our motel.

"Maybe we're just being stubborn, Demi," I mused as I thumbed idly through a local newspaper. Maybe *we're* the ones who want a farm and Jesus has something else in mind!"

I wasn't actually reading the paper before me—but

all of a sudden the words "Taxville Full Gospel Church" almost jumped from the page and hit me with a sharp sense of recognition. I'd never heard of that church before, but my spirit was rejoicing as if I'd suddenly seen an old friend.

"Demi!" I shouted. "Here it is! Here's the church that's going to help us!"

When I explained how my spirit was witnessing to that church, Demi thought I'd gone crazy, but he knew better than to argue with me. He took a blind step in faith with me and placed a call to the pastor of the Taxville Church. That phone call changed the course of our lives.

Chapter 30

NEW LIFE FOR GIRLS

Through that notice in the paper, the Holy Spirit had put us in touch with the Reverend Elwood Bell and his congregation of Spirit-filled Christians. This small country church became the first in York to give complete endorsement and support to our ministry. Mr. Bell was so excited about our proposed rehabilitation program for girls that he soon had us feeling as if he were the one who was asking a favor of *us*. His enthusiasm sent us back to New York in an entirely different frame of mind. The situation hadn't really changed, but we sensed a promise of something good to come.

In July, Mr. and Mrs. Bell, Pauline Bernstein, Demi, and I met in the Bell home to pray and share ideas and to select a name for our proposed ministry. We tried out many names—among them, "Outreach for Girls" and "Reaching Out for Girls"—but all agreed we'd hit just the right note with "New Life for Girls." Now that we had a name and the nucleus of a board of directors, it seemed time for our ministry to find a home.

The idea of a farm still had strong appeal for us, and Mrs. Bernstein agreed to survey all the farms being advertised for sale in the vicinity of York. We never really asked ourselves just how two Puerto Rican ex-drug-addicts with no jobs would manage to buy a piece of Pennsylvania farmland. We just knew that the time had come to take another step in faith. We were making weekly trips back and forth from New York City to York, often with Sylvia suffering the agony of withdrawal symptoms in the back seat of our car. She still had hopes of getting her life together and kicking her drug habit permanently, but without the help of a rehabilitation program she appeared to be fighting a losing battle. We tried to keep her with us as much as possible, but her old man and three daughters kept her tied to the life she was trying so hard to shed. As our commuting increased, we frequently had to take her along with us in whatever condition we found her. We knew time was running out for Sylvia, which only increased our sense of urgency for finding a farm. We were sure the Lord had a place in mind for this ministry.

In August came the phone call we had been praying for. Mrs. Bernstein had found a farm she thought we ought to see. "Cookie, it's just the right size—twenty-seven acres—and it's not far from York." My interest rose quickly.

"It has been a gentleman's farm," she continued, "—a kind of weekend retreat. And it has two small houses, a barn, a tool shed and even a swimming pool. Could you possibly—"

I never let her finish the sentence. I started crying with joy and shouting, "That's it! I just *know* that's the farm! New Life for Girls has found a home!"

We drove right out to see the property and claimed it at once for the Lord.

Claiming it was easy; paying for it was something else again. We had a grand total of $150 left from our earnings at Teen Challenge. All this sum could get us was a binder on the property. The farm was priced at $40,000, and $10,000 would be needed just for a down payment. To us, $10,000 sounded as bad as $1,000,-000. We redoubled our prayer efforts.

I still don't know where all that money came from! The Taxville Church, our friends in New York City, the Rettedals and Oldfields out in the Midwest—all gave us assistance. They planned meetings where we could share our dreams with other Christians. The trickle of love gifts and offerings began to grow into a small stream.

In September, we rented the smaller house on the farm property, and Demi and I—with our four children, Sylvia, and another girl named Aida—moved into it. We praised God that our days of commuting from New York were ended! Within two months after we moved, the Lord had provided the $10,000 we needed for the down payment on the farm. Our excitement was without limit. Feeling like millionaires, we went to the bank to talk business with their loan officer.

Again our hopes were dashed: the bank turned down our request for a mortgage. Even though we had the $10,000 needed for the down payment, we could not meet even the most basic requirements for a $30,000 mortgage. From a business point of view, a faith ministry with no apparent source of income is not a very sound investment! It appeared that we had reached a stalemate in our attempt to buy the farm.

We walked out of the bank in a daze. After the miraculous response of all those strangers to our testimony, after all the love gifts had poured in, we were so sure the Lord was leading us in this venture! But it appeared that we had been wrong. Weeping tears of frustration, we prayed and sought the Lord's will. "We were so close, Jesus! Don't You want us to buy our farm? What are You going to *do*, Lord?"

We had no resources of our own, but the Lord showed us again that nothing is impossible for Him.

At that point we had only sixty more days to come up with an acceptable financial arrangement or default on the binder and lose the option to purchase the property. For those two months we prayed for the Lord to find us another source of funding. With the deadline only a few days away, He revealed His answer to those prayers by prompting two of our York friends to offer us personal loans of $10,000 each. The Lord had worked another miracle! Once we had $30,000 in hand, the bank was willing to give us a mortgage for the remaining $10,000. Late in December, 1972, we became the legal owners of the farm. The Lord's gift to us that Christmas was a home for our new ministry. New Life for Girls had become a reality.

Just as the Lord had shown us how He could handle the purchase of His farm, He began at once to take charge of His rehabilitation program.

First He sent us the girls who needed our ministry. Starting with two girls, Sylvia and Aida, we soon had five—and then in no time double this number. When we felt that we could handle a maximum of twelve girls, we soon found that our total numbered seventeen! At the precise moment that we'd decide we were completely out of space, the Lord would show us a forgotten corner—the carport, for example. When enclosed by volunteer laborers, it accommodated six more girls. Another addition to the house gave some more girls a chance for a new life. We learned about trundle beds, and our capacity increased once again.

Recently we have had as many as twenty-six girls in the program at one time, and now we feel that the Lord wants us to build a dormitory for still more. We no longer talk in terms of limits. Our God is too big for such restrictions.

As He sent the girls to us, Jesus used each one to

teach us something new. For example, we finally learned the value of those work details and routines I'd disliked so much back at Rhinebeck. We had tried to minimize the rules and regulations, but the girls proved more relaxed and secure when the time was organized for them and they could follow a busy, detailed schedule.

Next He opened our eyes to the need for providing homes for the children of our girls. Sylvia's concern for her three girls whom she left with her mother in the New York ghetto reminded me of my own burden for Dondi when I was going through rehabilitation. At first we simply accepted help from Christian families in the surrounding community who offered to keep the children temporarily. Then a second, smaller farm became available for a low rental fee. This became home for New Life for Children, a ministry for the children of girls in our rehabilitation program. We have not completed our plans for this auxiliary ministry even yet, but we are striving to insure that no girl denies herself a new life because of her children.

Then He showed us clearly that a wide variety of girls needed Him. Although many girls came to us at first from the jail ministry, we soon had girls referred to us by various social agencies throughout the country. Some of our girls came from as far away as Minnesota and South Carolina, and some girls came from the York community. Furthermore some of the girls were black, some were white, and some were Puerto Rican. They all had the same basic need—to be put in touch with the Savior. They all wanted the new life that He promised. A few stayed a night, some stayed a week, and many—like Sylvia, and Aida, and Connie—just stayed.

The Lord also provided additional staff members as

they were needed with our growing program. From the Taxville Church we acquired a nurse and a counselor, and a secretary came forward from another church. From various drug programs operating elsewhere came other men and women with some knowledge of rehabilitation methods. One of the staff members He sent us this first year was Frances, who had just completed her rehabilitation program in New York. She stayed on as a counselor for several months before going back to minister in the street as she felt called to do. Because of Frances, Demi had decided to work with girls. Now Frances would be used to pass on the Lord's caring to others.

The Lord has continued to bless us with dedicated, self-sacrificing helpers. No matter what we have needed, the Lord has anticipated our needs and made the right provision for it.

He touched many individuals in the communities bordering the farm. He inspired one couple to supply milk for our program and led a businessman to offer electric typewriters for use in our office. He called one woman to tutor a Spanish-speaking girl in English and another to sew dresses for our new choir. It is impossible to describe all the ways in which the community responded to our work. At times it seemed that the Lord had moved on our behalf in all of York County at one time. Community arms spread wide to embrace us in a wonderful, warm Christian bear hug.

By the end of the first year on the farm we could look back to a year full of surprises and many good gifts from the hand of our bountiful Father. We had frequently been without financial resources, but we'd never been without His grace. And His grace had seen us through many crises.

In July, 1973—one year after our ministry had been

named—we dedicated the farm to His service. Two hundred friends of New Life for Girls came to the dedication service to praise God for establishing this ministry and for providing so well throughout the year. As we gathered around the site we are claiming for a new dormitory, we all shared a conviction that the Lord has many mighty miracles yet to accomplish through this ministry; and we rededicated ourselves to the task of being ready for whatever He might require from us.

Chapter 31

WHAT THE LORD HAS DONE

The crisp air seemed to promise snow on the December morning that Demi and I walked up the hill to the clearing where the much-desired dormitory would be constructed someday. The field seemed to shiver in the cold as we paused to stare longingly at the site. It had looked so different in July when we'd needed a tent to shelter our guests from the sun's heat at the dedication service.

The gray winter landscape did nothing to inspire dreams, but we were not seeing the field as it was. We were seeing it as it would be someday—filled with a cross-shaped building housing fifty to seventy-five girls and a chapel for the worship of the God Who had made it all possible. We could dream optimistically in the midst of an empty field because we knew that He had the power to fulfill these dreams. Look at what He'd already done in just one year.

Demi was looking at me and grinning, "I know what you're thinking."

I laughed as I responded, "That's not too tough—you're thinking the same thing. Won't it be grand when we can finally look at the completed building and say, 'Look what the Lord has done'? I can't believe all that He has done already in New Life For Girls!"

And both of us began to reminisce about the events that had led us to this place, about the first year of

New Life For Girls, and about how the Lord had blessed us all.

"Remember how pathetic Aida looked when she first came out here?" Demi began. "Hard to believe she was ever so frail and skinny!"

I had to smile. A mental picture of Aida as she had looked just a few days earlier at her "graduation" from the program flashed through my mind. No—our Aida was anything but skinny now! But it was true that no one had come to us in worse shape than she had. She had seemed all skin and bones and bruises and lice when we took her from the streets of New York City and brought her out to the farm. She had been taking a wild combination of cocaine, methadone, and barbiturates in addition to heroin, and the risk of convulsions was great. We were tempted to take her to a hospital to kick, but decided instead to trust Jesus with her. We drove straight to Pennsylvania. In a field beside the house we had cut her long filthy hair, and on her knees Aida had asked Jesus to come into her life. She'd kicked drugs without any convulsions and without much discomfort. We prayed with her through it all the way they had prayed for me at Clinton Avenue. Jesus did the rest!

Since Aida was one of the girls I had first ministered to in jail, she was very special to me. She was the kind of hard-core addict that Jesus had sent me to bring home to Him. And He had worked a special miracle for her once she had turned to Him for life. He had given her back her son. Joey had been raised in the home of Aida's mother, believing that Aida was his older sister. Aida had been so young when he was born that she had never been a mother to him. Like me, she began to long for normal family attachments once her life was straightened out by the Lord, and like me, she got her heart's desire. Joey accepted Aida

214

immediately as his mother and lives with her now at the farm. Through Aida and Joey, the Lord reminded us that nothing is impossible with Him. Even delicate psychological problems respond to His wisdom and love.

Each one of our girls had been used to teach us something special this first year. From Connie and Nadine we had learned that no one is too tough or too old for Jesus. Connie had been a homeless junkie for seventeen years before coming to New Life. Like me, she'd seen it all and done it all before she came to Jesus. Only she'd been at it much longer than any other girl I'd known until then. What a joy she had become! Connie is now a reliable, loving friend to all the girls— and she wants to go to school and return to New Life For Girls as a staff member! She would be such a valuable addition I am prepared to create a new position— Dean of Women—when she returns.

Nadine had shown us that Jesus wants to redeem "girls" of all ages. At forty-four years of age she sailed through the rehabilitation with ease and is now attending Bible school in preparation for Christian ministry to others like herself.

Then we'd learned that not all the lost girls are found in the ghetto. Peggy was not a hard-core addict and she was not a product of the New York slums, but she typified the exciting changes that Jesus brings in conferring new life. Peggy arrived at the farm early in the Fall, shortly after Sylvia and Aida. She was referred to us by a Christian social worker in Minnesota. When we first met she was twenty-three years old and considered incorrigible by all who knew her. She was born to a family of very modest means in the Midwest, but she had been reared in the Christian faith by a believing mother. Nevertheless she had entered an endless round of rebellion as a teen-ager and could not find her way out of the mire into which she had fallen. She'd been married at a young age but was separated from her husband. When she came to the farm she brought with her two children—a red-haired boy of three and a half, and a tiny blonde daughter just two and a half. She also brought with her memories of a past which included years of sexual abuse, marijuana and barbiturate usage, alcohol, and child abuse. Like Aida she was malnourished and not at all optimistic about her chances for surviving in rehabilitation. But survive she *did!*

A wonderful family in a nearby community took the children in hand and shared their abundant love with them. In spite of the poor start they'd had, they blossomed into healthy, active youngsters with a normal zest for living.

Peggy had blossomed too. She'd filled out nicely on three meals a day and become the red-haired beauty she'd been concealing all those years. But best of all, she had drawn so close to her Lord that her personality was totally changed. She became a shy but loving girl whose quiet, steady ways gave her a dignity that we'd never seen in her before.

Peggy had not needed a full twelve-month rehabilitation program to get her life in order. She was "graduated" after seven months and went back to Minnesota to work in a rehabilitation ministry.

I guess I could have spent hours on such thoughts as these. The girls had been inspirational to us as well as to each other. Girls like Ginny, who had come to us with unflagging determination to succeed, made our job all the easier; but even the ones who couldn't stay had left us with some new insight. Girls like Marie and Naomi, and even Frances, our counselor, had taught us lessons we needed to learn. From Frances we had learned that the lives of our girls may take a direction

216

we'd not planned upon ourselves. The Lord wanted us to know that only He can direct the new lives He gives to His children.

I looked over at Demi, who was reading my thoughts as usual. "We've learned a lot, haven't we?" he asked. And we still have a long way to go! Hasn't the Lord been good to us to keep teaching us all along the way? I'd sure hate to take on the crowd we have down there today with some of the half-baked notions we had when we first got here."

I knew what he meant. We'd started out our ministry to the girls with nothing to offer but the love and power we knew was found in Jesus—a great place to start, of course, but that hardly constituted a rehabilitation program. Then we had added daily worship services, Bible study, and work details until we gradually discovered principles and techniques that could be applied in bringing discipline to these unruly girls. We discovered, for example, that the girls themselves were the most successful in praying with a girl who was kicking. The counselors who had never been addicted just weren't as useful in that particular way.

I looked over at Demi, who was again gazing at the frozen field, and felt a peace and love that surpassed mere human emotion.

"Honey," he said as he turned toward me then, "Let's go back down to the house. You're looking cold." He slid his arm around me and turned me toward the path. "I bet it's going to snow. Can't you just hear the kids when they see this hill covered? They'll be wanting sleds for Christmas."

I took another look over my shoulder at the empty field, then fell into step with him as we went back down the hill to the office, where business went on as usual. "Do you really think we'll ever have that dormitory, Demi? We're not being too greedy, are we—to want something that grand for our girls?"

"Are you kidding? Look how the Lord has blessed this work already. Who do you think is sending us all those girls? Look—He wants His girls taken care of. And whatever He does, He does right."

"Of course! How could I ever forget!" My mind traveled back over all that God had done for me—how He had saved my life, even before I knew Him, and kept me from having that twenty-year jail sentence. He had sent Nicky and Gloria Cruz to minister to me; and when I wouldn't receive their witness, He had not given up—He had sent One-Eyed Dutch to lead me to Teen Challenge. He had come into my heart, filled me with His Holy Spirit, trained me in His work, and even sent me to Bible school. He had given me Demi— and with him, the family I had always wanted and never had. Just thinking about His goodness brought tears to my eyes. Tears! That was another thing.

I could cry.

PRONUNCIATION OF SPANISH TERMS

ABUELITA (ab-wua-LEE-ta): little grandmother.
BARRIO (BAH-ree-o): ghetto.
BOMBITAS (bom-BEE-tas): amphetamines.
CAGUAS (KA-gways): Cookie's home town in Puerto Rico.
CAGUITA (Ka-GWEE-ta): "Little Caguas."
VELADA (ve-LAH-dah): a seance. Las Veladas: "the seances."

GLOSSARY OF STREET SLANG

BUST: arrest. (Used as either a verb or a noun, as in "There was a bust," or "He got busted.")
COLD TURKEY: suddenly breaking a drug habit without the use of other drugs. Named after the gooseflesh, a common symptom of withdrawal.
DEB: a girl gang member; the girlfriend of a gang member.
DOWNERS: depressants.
FIX: an injection of narcotics.
HIGH: under the influence of drugs.
JUNK: narcotics, especially heroin.
KICK: to break a drug habit.

LITTLE PUERTO RICO: Spanish Harlem. The area east of Fifth Avenue—including First, Second, Third, and Madison Avenues and Lexington—the heart of which is around 110th Street.

MAINLINING: injecting drugs intravenously.

MIND HABIT: a mental addiction to drugs which often remains even after the physical dependence has been broken.

NOD: to be sleepy from narcotics.

OD: a drug overdose. One who has taken a drug overdose. Used as either a verb or a noun, as in "He ODed," or "He took an OD."

OLD LADY: somebody's mother. Also, the woman a man lives with.

OLD MAN: somebody's father. Also, the man a woman lives with.

PANIC: a shortage of heroin.

POT: marijuana.

POTHEAD: heavy marijuana user.

SCORE: make a drug purchase.

SET: a party.

SHOOTING GALLERY: place where addicts go to inject drugs.

SKIN POPPING: intramuscular (as opposed to intravenous) injection of drugs.

SNORT: to take drugs (esp. heroin or cocaine) by sniffing them into the nose.

TAKE OFF: to steal, as in "to take someone off for something." Today, street people use the expression "rip off" to mean the same thing.

TRACKS: (also, railroad tracks) scars along the vein after many injections. So named because of their appearance.

TREY: a three-dollar bag of heroin.

TRICK: a prostitute's customer.

TURF: a gang's territory.

UPPERS: stimulants.

WAR COUNSELOR: gang official in charge of negotiations concerning fights.

WEST HARLEM: the section west of Fifth Avenue, also including Broadway and Lenox Avenue and extending roughly from 110th Street up to 155th Street.

ZIP GUN: a gun fashioned out of wood and fired by a rubber band, sometimes having a regular gun "works" inside.